THE JOY OF FOOTBALL

JOHNNY MORGAN

summersdale

THE JOY OF FOOTBALL

Summersdale Publishers Ltd
46 West Street
Chichester
West Sussex
PO19 1RP
UK

www.summersdale.com

Printed and bound in the Czech Republic

ISBN: 978-1-84953-600-4

Substantial discounts on bulk quantities of Summersdale books are available to corporations, professional associations and other organisations. For details contact Nicky Douglas by telephone: +44 (0) 1243 756902, fax: +44 (0) 1243 786300 or email: nicky@summersdale.com.

For Tom

I would like to thank Mum and Dad, for the footballs, kits, boots, stickers, tickets, magazines, games and everything else.

Thanks also to Sarah, for your patience with and feeding of this continuing obsession, and to Gregg and Ben, for the help only similarly addicted souls can provide.

CONTENTS

INTRODUCTION

The great fallacy is that the game is first and last about winning. It's nothing of the kind. The game is about glory. It is about doing things in style, with a flourish, about going out and beating the other lot, not waiting for them to die of boredom.

TOTTENHAM HOTSPUR LEGEND
DANNY BLANCHFLOWER

The joy of football? Where do I start? I don't think I can point a finger at one single thing – it's many things to many people. It's something deeply personal but at the same time shared, often intimately, with millions of others. It is tribal yet universal, everyday yet special, crushing yet utterly thrilling.

There is nothing like playing the game. Five-a-side, seven-a-side, 11-a-side, it doesn't matter. Of course, the joy is in scoring goals, tackling, making passes or pulling off saves, but it's also in pulling on the shirt, wearing your clubs' colours and trying to emulate your heroes. It's about going collectively into battle, pitting yourself against your opponents, giving everything you have and finding out if it's enough. Whether you're playing in the local park, in the evening for your work team or on Saturday or Sunday in a weekend league, when you play well, when it all comes off, when you score, when you win, there is no feeling quite like it. It's immense, whatever age you are.

Then there's watching the game, whether it's in the stands or on the television. Arriving at the stadium, picking up a programme, getting a drink and a snack, finding your seat and watching the action unfold before your eyes: it's a ritual that has a soul-stirring electricity and one that fans repeat religiously for a lifetime. Why do they keep doing the same thing? Partly because each game is a step into the unknown. That's the joy right there. This is what keeps us turning up, at the turnstile, at the pub or on the sofa. You can never be sure of what is going to happen: lucky bounces, cruel deflections, yellow cards, early baths, last-minute winners, last-minute misses. Who will be heroes and who will be villains? That's what it boils down to: good against evil. It's *Star Wars* but each club gets the chance to write its own script.

And the final draft of that script is another place where the joy of football can be found. When you can't be playing or watching football, there is another way to get your hit: by reading about it. Poring over match reports, digesting the stats, seeing how a day's matches have affected your teams and others, working out who's closer to glory and whose fate looks ever more doomed. That's why the papers are full of football pages, why there are countless football magazines, websites and podcasts. And it's not just the latest games; football history is a treasure chest waiting to be opened, inside the prospect of finding something new and wonderful every time, whether it's a look back at a past player, a classic game, a great manager or a winning philosophy. This is a well that, it seems, will never run dry.

Reading (and watching) also leads us to different worlds. The globalisation of the game in the past 30 years has been incredible and this revolution has given us access to football in foreign lands, both on screen and in print. It has given us the chance to discover how the game on our doorstep is so different yet so similar to that played on faraway pitches. Today football on the other side of the world is just as close as football at the other end of the street.

Playing, watching and reading: three good places to start when it comes to unearthing the ingredients that make up the joy of football. But there is more, obviously: collecting replica tops, scarves and stickers are just a few more hobbies of the hopelessly addicted. Of course, I should also mention writing about football. All fans do it in some way or another, whether it's by messaging friends, posting on Internet forums or writing blogs, it's just another excuse to show your love for the game.

CHAPTER 1

A BRIEF HISTORY OF FOOTBALL

Football, bloody hell!
SIR ALEX FERGUSON

When did it all begin? Who gets credit for inventing the beautiful game? Well, that isn't entirely clear. There's mention of *tsu chu*, involving a leather ball filled with feathers and hair, in China around 200 BC; *kemari*, which featured players standing in a small circle trying to keep the ball off the ground, in Japan in AD 600; *episkyros*, a much more physical pursuit than its Far Eastern equivalent, at roughly the same time in Greece; something called Shrovetide football, akin to mob football where hands were used as much as feet, in the Middle Ages in England; and *calcio*, comprising 27 players whose focus was fighting as much as football, in Italy in the 1500s. Let's just say it's a global game. But one thing is certain: the modern game, as we know it, was born in 1863. The fun hasn't stopped since.

A timeline of modern football

1862	Notts County, the oldest professional football club, is formed
1863	The rules of Association Football are drawn up in England
1869	Goal kicks are introduced to the game
1870	The position of goalkeeper is officially recognised
1872	Corner kicks are introduced to the game
1872	The first international takes place; Scotland play England
1874	Shin pads are introduced and teams change ends at half time
1877	The duration of a match is set at 90 minutes
1890	Goal nets are used for the first time
1891	Penalty kicks are introduced
1893	The first three-figure transfer: Willie Groves to Aston Villa for £100
1904	FIFA is founded in Paris
1923	The first FA Cup final at Wembley: Bolton v. West Ham
1930	The first World Cup takes place in Uruguay
1937	Football is televised for the first time: highlights of Arsenal v. Arsenal Reserves

1939	Shirt numbering becomes compulsory
1951	The use of a white ball is permitted for the first time
1960	The European Championship is founded
1960	The first live English Football League game is broadcast on TV
1965	Substitutions are permitted in the English Football League
1970	The game sees its first red and yellow cards
1979	Trevor Francis becomes the first British £1-million footballer
1991	The first women's football World Cup in China
1992	The English Premier League is born
1992	The Champions League replaces the European Cup
2002	The World Cup takes place in Asia for the first time
2010	The World Cup takes place in Africa for the first time
2012	Goal-line technology is used for the first time
2014	Vanishing spray (to mark the correct position for defensive walls) is used for the first time at a World Cup

A level playing field

LAWS OF THE GAME

While football had existed in various forms for centuries, it wasn't very organised. Steps had to be taken to turn the chaos into something more cultured, into a spectacle that was fairer, and whose joy could be shared far and wide. Association Football was the result, with the first laws drawn up in 1863 with the purpose of 'embracing the true principles of the game, with the greatest simplicity'.

When Preston ruled the world

The first football league competition was held in England between the autumn of 1888 and the spring of 1889, and Preston North End dominated it completely. The Lilywhites, as their fans call them, were on top of the world – they were invincible, unbeaten over the entire 22-game season. They won the year after, too. Since then, things haven't been quite so good, but they'll always have that season in the sun.

And what a season it was. It took until 2003–04 for another team, Arsenal, to emulate Preston and go a whole English Football League season without loss. The Gunners had to play nearly twice as many games, but let's not get bogged down in detail. The Lilywhites were one of the 12 founding fathers of the league and you can only beat what's put in front of you, and that they did. They put seven past Stoke City and five past Burnley, Derby County and Wolverhampton Wanderers at home, and seven past Brighton & Hove Albion on the road. Two Preston players led the top scorers' table, with John Goodall just pipping teammate James Ross thanks to a goal-a-game record.

Incredibly, Preston won the FA Cup in the same season, becoming the first English team to claim the coveted Double. They did it without conceding a goal, too. They rattled three past Bootle, two past Grimsby Town, two more past Birmingham City and one past West Bromwich Albion, before beating Wolves 3–0 in the final at the Kennington Oval in London in front of over 27,000 fans. How do the Arsenal Invincibles compare? They lost in the semi-finals. Close, but no cigar.

ENGLAND MANAGER ALF RAMSEY TO STRIKER RODNEY MARSH:
If you don't work harder I'll pull you off at half time.

SOON TO BE EX-ENGLAND STRIKER TO ENGLAND MANAGER ALF RAMSEY:
Crikey, Alf, at Manchester City all we get is an orange and a cup of tea.

The second coming

Talk to fans of a certain age group and you'd think that football didn't exist before the advent of the Premier League. Before this juggernaut came rumbling into view, there was just darkness, lurking in which were horrors such as really short shorts, mullets and limited media coverage.

It's not true, obviously, but the Premier League did usher in a new era of football and, with the help of a sports channel belonging to a certain Australian media tycoon, turned it into the behemoth we look upon today. And it's not just a British we: visit Asia or Africa and the streets will be awash with the shirts of Manchester United, Liverpool, Arsenal, Chelsea and others. There's a reason for that: the rise and rise of the Premier League.

Before 1992, watching football on television wasn't always so easy. The number of televised games was limited to one or two a week, if you were lucky, and as far as highlights went, you had to pay attention to the listings and hunt down specific programmes at certain times to get a glimpse of the action. And if your team was playing in the week, watching the match took some serious dedication and the ability to stay up late (past the greyhound racing and showjumping). You couldn't just turn on the box and breezily flick around until you found something you wanted to watch. Four or five top-flight games over a weekend? Super Saturday? Super Sunday? Monday Night Football? For that kind of joy you had to wait for the World Cup.

The make-up of English football has changed in other ways since the arrival of the Premier League. The extra money has enabled more and more domestic clubs to look further afield for talent and they have grabbed this opportunity with both hands: the league now has the second-largest proportion of overseas players in Europe (Cyprus is first). The merits of this evolution are much debated: for all the Cantonas, Zolas, Henrys and Bergkamps, there are the Boogerses, Bogardes, Bebés and Brolins. Furthermore, the England team hasn't been much cop of late, a decline which some argue is a result of the lack of opportunity for young home-grown players. Nevertheless, it has created an insatiable appetite around the world for the league.

Talking of hunger, the influx of Premier League riches means that today top footballers become millionaires almost overnight. Not too long ago, the footballing wage was largely a modest one: in 1958, the maximum a footballer could earn was £20 a week, now Wayne Rooney gets paid £300,000 a week. Transfer fees have also gone through the ceiling: from £1 million for Trevor Francis in 1979 to £50 million for Fernando Torres in 2011. And let's not forget more recent moves such as £44 million for Mesut Özil, £39.5 million for Sergio Aguero and £37.5 million for Juan Mata.

So, in a way, 1992 was year zero: before that it was a game that a lot of fans would no longer recognise.

What a goal!

The first Premier League goal was scored by Brian Deane for Sheffield United against Manchester United in 1992. The Blades beat the Red Devils 2–1.

The 10,000th Premier League goal was scored by Les Ferdinand for Tottenham Hotspur against Fulham in 2001.

The 20,000th Premier League goal was scored by Marc Albrighton for Aston Villa against Arsenal in 2011.

CHAPTER 2

GREAT FOOTBALLING RIVALRIES

There are two great teams on Merseyside;
Liverpool and Liverpool Reserves.
BILL SHANKLY

Where would football be without the bitter rivalries, the timeless feuds or the great grudges? It wouldn't be nearly as much fun. Every country has its big showdowns: Real Madrid and Barcelona in Spain, AC and Inter Milan in Italy, Boca Juniors and River Plate in Argentina, but nobody does it quite like the English, especially when it comes to international football.

V.

England versus Scotland

While a decline in the standard of Scottish football has dimmed the profile of this game in recent times, the intensity that surrounds it remains as fierce as ever. Asked who he would support at the 2010 World Cup, Scotland's Andy Murray replied 'anyone but England', which tells you all you need to know.

England against Scotland was the first international match ever to be played, with the inaugural showdown taking place in 1872. The final score was 0–0, with few fireworks to report, but all that would change. Over time, each team would hand out a shellacking or two to the other, but few were as fearful as the 9–3 victory inflicted by England in 1961, which reportedly helped the Scottish goalkeeper decide to emigrate to Australia.

However, revenge would be sweet for the Tartan Army. Fresh from its finest hour, Alf Ramsey's World Cup winners took on Scotland at the old Wembley in 1967. Full of swagger, England were massive favourites and seemingly certain of victory. But they were beaten 3–2 and the Scots claimed possibly their most famous triumph. Somewhat cheekily, they crowned themselves unofficial champions of the world.

Ten years later, England against Scotland made the headlines again, although the football had little to do with it. By this time, England were in the doldrums having failed to reach an international tournament since 1970 (a run that would continue until 1980) and Scotland were enjoying a purple patch. It is hard to imagine that their supporters didn't take every opportunity to remind the English about it. Still, their celebrations after a 2–1 win in London remain infamous to this day. The Tartan Army invaded the pitch, tearing it up as they went and using the goalposts as monkey bars, eventually snapping one set in half.

In the wake of this match, England against Scotland became a marked game, with authorities ever more concerned over the likelihood of violence. In 1989, it disappeared from the international calendar, not to be seen for seven years. However, as the Madness song goes, you can't keep a good thing down and when the game did return, it was in some style.

England was hosting the 1996 European Championship and the team were drawn against Scotland in their group. The old rivalry was back on, the heat was turned back up again and the fans got a game to savour. The pivotal moment saw Scotland's captain Gary McAllister miss a penalty and England's Paul Gascoigne (better known as Gazza) head straight up the other end to put his team 2–0 up with one of the goals of the tournament. For a moment, the Three Lions had their supporters believing football was coming home.

Footie Fact

Scotland have played at eight World Cups, but actually qualified for nine. Having qualified for the 1950 tournament in Sweden, the Scottish FA refused to let the team go because they weren't the British champions. Hubris 1 common sense 0.

England versus Germany

> *Football is a simple game; 22 men chase a ball for*
> *90 minutes and at the end the Germans win.*
>
> GARY LINEKER

Germany is another of England's famous footballing foes. England may have beaten the Tartan Army at Euro 96, but they wouldn't get the best of another arch rival later in the competition: English dreams were crushed mercilessly by Germany in the semi-final and it was a feeling that was all too familiar for the English.

So where did it all start to go wrong for England when it came to playing Germany? The 4–2 victory over West Germany in 1966 is the high point to which English football has never returned. Things started to take a turn for the worse in the blazing heat of Mexico in 1970. England were the reigning world champions and, with arguably a stronger side, they were confident of defending their crown. Progressing to the quarter-finals, England were pitted against the West Germans once again and, 2–0 up after 50 minutes, they looked on course to record another victory. However, it was not to be: the stand-in goalie Peter Bonetti made a massive blunder and striker Jeff Aston missed an absolute sitter, and the game finished 3–2 in the West Germans' favour.

And, so England's stupor began. It wasn't until 1982 that the team returned to the World Cup and it wasn't until 1990 that they got close to a final again. After a bad start, England found some rhythm and squeaked through to the semi-finals, where they faced a familiar foe. All England fans will know what happened next: a quite incredible game tipped one way and the other, West Germany scored, Lineker equalised, Gazza cried, it went to penalties and German ruthlessness won the day.

If that defeat left England fans heartbroken, then the result of the semi-final at Euro 96 inflicted some serious mental scars, not only concerning playing the Germans but also taking penalties. Again, the game was a tight affair and, in front of their home fans, England looked to avenge that painful night in Turin. But it didn't happen: penalties decided the tie again, and again England came up short, with Gareth Southgate joining Chris Waddle and Stuart Pearce in England's penalty hall of shame. Not that they would be alone for long – many others would follow.

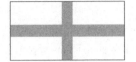 **v.**

England versus Argentina

One of the displays of abject penalty-taking by England that followed the losses in 1990 and 1996 was against Argentina in the 1998 World Cup. Paul Ince and David Batty would be ushered into the unfortunate pantheon of England players to mess up from 12 yards. The chance to avenge an infamous defeat was spurned.

Like the feud with Germany, England's beef with Argentina goes back to 1966. The events of a quarter-final game between the two sides sparked a fierce rivalry that continues to this day. England won 1-0 thanks to a Geoff Hurst goal, but it was the sending off of the Argentinian captain Antonio Rattín that would cause the bad blood. Reports vary regarding the reason for Rattín's dismissal, but, in the end, so furious was the player that he had to be escorted from the pitch by the police. The Argentinians were labelled animals, and the press and public at home were duly outraged.

They say that revenge is a dish best served cold - and it doesn't get much colder than 30 years later, in the form of one of the most infamous incidents the World Cup has ever seen. Diego Maradona's 'Hand of God' in the quarter-final of the 1986 World Cup in Mexico has gone down in the tournament's history, and despite the fact that he scored one of the best goals ever seen at a World Cup later in the game, and that his imperious team would go on to lift the trophy, it was an act that few English fans have been able to forget or forgive. But for Argentinian fans simmering over the injustice of 1966, and the Falklands War in 1982, it didn't matter in the slightest. The English press got itself into an unholy funk, but for Argentina, karma had come calling and England were conquered when it mattered the most.

The 1998 World Cup in France offered England a chance to exorcise this particular demon, but David Beckham's red card, along with the inability of his teammates to muster a victory from 12 yards, meant that the Three Lions had to wait longer for some closure. The opportunity came again in 2002, this time at the World Cup co-hosted by Japan and South Korea, where the two sides faced each other at the group stage and, for once, England didn't pass it up. Beckham scored from the penalty spot, gaining redemption for the events of four years earlier, England won 1–0 and Argentina exited the tournament early.

Footie Fact

In 1978, Sheffield United arranged to sign a 17-year-old Maradona for £200,000, but had to pull out of the deal because they couldn't afford it.

CHAPTER 3

THE WORLD CUP

Good afternoon. Shouldn't you be at work?
BBC PRESENTER DES LYNAM'S FIRST WORDS TO THE CAMERA WHEN INTRODUCING
ENGLAND'S GAME AGAINST TUNISIA AT THE 1998 WORLD CUP. KICK OFF TIME? 2 P.M.

The English Premier League, La Liga in Spain, the Bundesliga in Germany, the UEFA Champions League: they have the football, the stars, glamour and the money, but the World Cup still trumps them all. For one month every four years, the world eats, sleeps and breathes football.

The World Cup begins

Unsurprisingly the World Cup has changed a lot since its grand launch in 1930. The inaugural tournament in Uruguay bears little resemblance to the meticulously organised, super-sponsored competitions we consume today. For a start, teams were hardly falling over themselves to play. For all the success of the Olympic football tournaments in the 1920s and the efforts of FIFA President Jules Rimet, who threw all his energy behind creating a global competition for his organisation, no one wanted to take part. It's fair to say that the World Cup got off to a slow start.

Everyone at FIFA got excited, the competition was announced a good two years in advance of when it would actually be played and the invitations were sent out. So far so good, except FIFA hadn't counted on a somewhat sniffy reaction from Europe's football associations. Initially, everyone said thanks, but no thanks. The cost of travel was the widely cited excuse, but the reason for the lacklustre response wasn't entirely financial: the Home Nations were mired in a period of arch snobbery and felt the competition was beneath them.

Eventually some arm-twisting from Rimet resulted in four teams making the trip: Belgium, France, Romania and Yugoslavia. They joined Argentina, Bolivia, Brazil, Chile, Mexico, Paraguay, Peru and the USA, as well as the hosts Uruguay, who were all, unsurprisingly, keener to make the much shorter journey. The tournament was played by 13 teams across three venues, all in the capital Montevideo, and comprised 18 games, with Uruguay defeating Argentina 2–1 in the final 17 days after the first ball had been kicked. Compare this with 2014: 32 teams, 12 venues across a very large country, 64 games and 31 days.

It would take a while before the English FA got over themselves, the South Americans got over being snubbed by the Europeans (there were retaliatory boycotts in 1934 and 1938) and teams stopped pulling out for sometimes spurious reasons (Olympic football is more important, we don't want to wear football boots, etc.). But by 1982, the World Cup was expanded to 24 teams and in 1998 to 32, by which time the tournament was truly a global affair that everyone took seriously.

Will the World Cup get any bigger? Arguably it doesn't need to, but common sense has long been out of fashion when considering such things. A 40-team tournament has been eagerly discussed by FIFA and UEFA, so expect it to happen one day soon.

Footie Fact

Brazil is the fifth country to host the World Cup for a second time, following Italy (1934 and 1990), France (1938 and 1998), Mexico (1970 and 1986) and Germany (1974 as West Germany and 2006).

The winners take it all

Winning and losing. The joy of victory and the fear of defeat. What else is the World Cup, or indeed any football tournament about? That's why we watch, even if it means getting up in the middle of the night or pleading with the boss to get out of work early.

When it comes to being joyful, it's the Brazilian fans who have the most reasons to be happy, not just because of the way their team play the game (or used to at least), but because they've walked off with football's ultimate crown a record five times, even before hosting the tournament again in 2014. Plus they're the only side to win it on four different continents.

Of course Brazil isn't the only team to have multiple World Cup notches on its bedpost. Argentina and Uruguay have both won it twice, while West Germany triumphed three times and Italy can boast four victories. And it shouldn't be forgotten that England, France and Spain have all brought the big one home once. Notably, England and France were both victorious as hosts and history has shown that putting on the party does improve your chances. Apart from the home victories in 1966 and 1998, the hosts have won it on four other occasions. That's not a bad ratio; still, Qatari fans shouldn't get too excited about 2022.

The very best of losers

Just as there are big winners, there are also big losers. The Ferenc Puskás-led Hungarian team dominated the world of football in the 1950s, but failed to claim the big prize. The Magical Magyars came closest in 1954: they blasted their way to the final before succumbing, in controversial circumstances, to West Germany, a team they had already thrashed earlier in the tournament.

The Netherlands are another side that somehow have no World Cup wins to show for all the hugely gifted players (Johan Cruyff, Marco van Basten, Ruud Gullit, Dennis Bergkamp, Robin van Persie, etc.) and the dazzling talent they have displayed. The Dutch were desperately unlucky to finish second best to West Germany in 1974 and Argentina in 1978, but only had themselves to blame in 2010 after their strategy of trying to kick Spain into submission failed and they had to settle for the runner-up spot for a third time.

```
      SPAIN 1982 WORLD CUP
   EL SALVADOR            1
           HUNGARY        10
```

The heaviest defeat suffered at a World Cup? Hungary beat El Salvador 10-1 in Spain in 1982. South Korea (who lost 9-0 to Hungary in 1954) and Zaire (who lost 9-0 to Yugoslavia in 1974) probably felt just as bad.

Most Top 8 World Cup Finishes

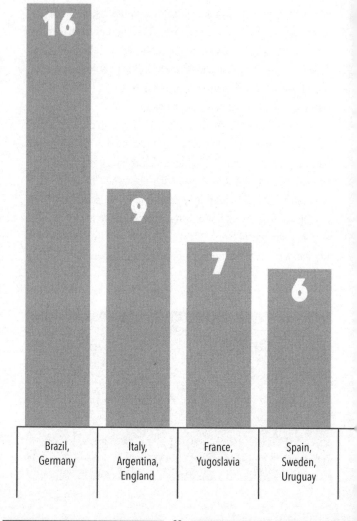

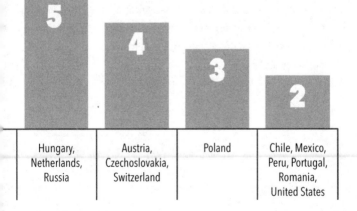

Hungary, Netherlands, Russia	Austria, Czechoslovakia, Switzerland	Poland	Chile, Mexico, Peru, Portugal, Romania, United States
5	4	3	2

Star light, star bright

Who are the stars of the World Cup? OK, we might remember how the likes of Franz Beckenbauer (he of God-like status, if you're German, and maybe even if you're not), Roger Milla (him of Cameroon and the fancy dance) and Gazza (oh the skill, oh the tears) lit up tournaments in their time, but when it comes down to it, it's the goals that count, and in particular the players who scored the most.

Beckenbauer and Milla may have notched up a fair few goals between them (both with a very respectable five), but the daddy of hitting the back of the net at the World Cup is Ronaldo. Not the new, slick version, but the older, cuddlier one. He banged in 15 goals for Brazil, which is one more than Miroslav Klose, although the German striker was still plying his trade, as they say, in the run up to the 2014 tournament. Behind these guys are Just Fontaine of France, with 13, and Pelé, with 12.

So, does being a top World Cup goal-scorer make you one of the best of all time? Quite possibly, but such a judgement is perhaps an impossible one to make. To score a goal in a World Cup you have to actually be there: there are plenty of players whose skills are lauded as some of the best the sport has seen, but who have never graced the game's ultimate tournament.

Take George Best for instance. For all his proclivities off the field, on it he was near peerless, but being a Northern Irishman his opportunities to prove himself on the biggest stage were next to none. Ryan Giggs is another player whose mercurial skills were never given the World Cup showcase they deserved. His Wales teams toiled away at qualification but could never drag themselves over the finishing line, even with the help of their Welsh Wizard.

Footie Fact

Robert Prosinečki is the only player to have scored World Cup goals for two different countries. For Yugoslavia in 1990 and Croatia in 1998.

Of course, such a fate is not solely a British phenomenon. European football has its own stories of this type of poor fortune, and none perhaps as unfortunate as that of Alfredo Di Stéfano. Di Stéfano is a footballing god, grouped by many among the game's very best (we're talking Pelé, Maradona and Messi territory here). The reason, perhaps, why he isn't automatically included at this top table is because he never played in a World Cup. It wasn't for lack of trying, although it was arguably the trying that did for him. Before he even arrived at Real Madrid in 1953, where he went on to win five European Cups, the Argentinian striker had already turned out for his native country and Colombia. A mixture of non-qualification, withdraws and bans kept him from World Cups. So, he switched his allegiance to Spain (who knows what was going on at FIFA), but Scotland (yes, Scotland) blocked his path in 1958 and he was injured in 1962. And that was it: three countries and no World Cup.

The book on such players can't be closed without mention of George Weah. He was another sublimely gifted player – the 1995 FIFA World Player of the Year – from Liberia. As far as World Cups go that's a major problem right there. Can you name another Liberian player? Did you know Liberia even had a team? Exactly. Liberia has never come close to qualification and neither did poor old George.

CHAPTER 4

THE DARK SIDE
OF THE BALL

I wasn't refereeing, I was acting as an umpire in military manoeuvres.
KEN ASTON ON HIS EXPERIENCE AS THE REFEREE OF THE 1962 BATTLE OF SANTIAGO

The beautiful game; sometimes it isn't so beautiful. Sometimes the handbags become properly argy-bargy. Sometimes football games are like wars. Sometimes they start wars.

The Battle of Santiago

The 1960s was a time of peace and love, but both these sentiments were in very short supply during the match between Chile and Italy at the 1962 World Cup. A metaphorical fire had already been lit under the game – Chile, as hosts, had struggled to prepare for the tournament following the Valdivia earthquake and a couple of Italian journalists had mercilessly laid into the state of the capital Santiago, making a song and dance about some perceived inadequacies. So incensed were the locals that the two hacks had to leave the country for their own safety. To no one's great surprise, as soon as the whistle was blown the game didn't take very long to explode: the first foul was committed after a matter of seconds, followed swiftly by a sending off after just 12 minutes. The culprit, the Italian Giorgio Ferrini, refused to go and had to be escorted from the pitch, kicking and screaming, by the police.

From there on in, the game slowly descended into violent farce with retaliation following retaliation. Mario David was the second and, unfathomably, the last man to get an early bath, for a flying kick to the head of Chile's Alexis Sánchez. In David's defence, Sánchez had not long before dropped him with a left hook. Sánchez wasn't finished either – he broke the nose of another Italian player later in the game. A football game did break out briefly, albeit with Italy having only nine men. Needless to say it was Chile that won. No wonder the English referee Ken Aston went on to invent the yellow and red cards.

Footie Fact

Marco Materazzi, famously headbutted by Zinedine Zidane in the 2006 World Cup final, played a single season in the English Premier League. In just 27 appearances for Everton, he picked up three red cards and 12 yellows. That's some going.

The Battle of Nuremberg

If the Battle of Nuremberg in 2006, featuring Holland and Portugal at the World Cup in Germany, teaches us one lesson, it's that football isn't very good at learning lessons. The advent of televised football and its growth into a global phenomenon has arguably made players a little more wary of committing out and out GBH on a football pitch – the Battle of Santiago was in some ways an end of an era – but the Dutch and Portuguese players contesting this Round-of-16 game seemed to undergo some collective brain freeze, kicking each other (and occasionally a ball) around the pitch for 90 bruising minutes.

Holland's Mark van Bommel set the tone after just two minutes, before teammate Khalid Boulahrouz well and truly ignited the blue touch paper with a murderous challenge on a young Cristiano Ronaldo, which put an end to the Portuguese's game. From there on in the tackles came thick and fast, most of which were late, high or both. By the time the final whistle went, it was a nine-a-side game whose Russian referee had managed to dish out 16 yellow cards in addition to the two red ones, which is a World Cup record.

The Football War

Did the World Cup qualifying matches between El Salvador and Honduras in 1969 start the Football War? Well, yes and no. Relations between the two countries were already at breaking point thanks to trade, land and immigration issues, but the three games between the two sides proved the tipping point.

In hindsight, the last thing that needed to happen was a large-scale display of nationalism. But, of course, it did and the results were predictably incendiary. The febrile atmosphere and violence that engulfed the ties was the spark that brought the two countries into open conflict. The decisive third game (held in neutral Mexico) – each side had won one match before that – hadn't even taken place before El Salvador broke off diplomatic relations with Honduras. Just over two weeks after they had booked their place at the World Cup, they had invaded their neighbours. The war lasted just 100 hours and El Salvador's World Cup only three matches, in which they failed to bother the scoresheet once.

The mark of a (footballing) man

Violence in football isn't always a team affair. Sometimes it can be a solo act. The history of the game is littered with the boneheaded actions of individual players, whether committed against opponents, teammates, officials or fans. But there are those that have left a bigger mark than others.

Flipping the birds

One of the most infamous acts of on-field thuggery in the modern game didn't happen on the pitch at all. For all his sublime skill and winners' medals, Eric Cantona is remembered by many for 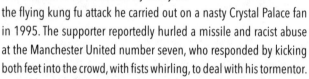 the flying kung fu attack he carried out on a nasty Crystal Palace fan in 1995. The supporter reportedly hurled a missile and racist abuse at the Manchester United number seven, who responded by kicking both feet into the crowd, with fists whirling, to deal with his tormentor.

While the Frenchman received some sympathy from within the game, the authorities were anything but understanding. Cantona was initially handed a two-week jail sentence, which was eventually reduced to 120 hours of community service, and the FA banned him for nine months and fined him £20,000. For good measure, the French FA stripped him of the captaincy of the national side and chucked him out of the team. For Cantona, it was a heavy price to pay for losing his famously fiery temper, but there was a silver lining of sorts: the game did get one of its best quotes of all time:

When the seagulls follow the trawler, it's because they think sardines will be thrown into the sea. Thank you very much.
Eric Cantona's cryptic response to his punishment

Quick to bite

When you hear a commentator say that a player is quick to bite, 99 times of 100 he means that the person in question has a short temper and can be easily riled. But what about that other time? That time is Luis Suárez.

In a game deflated by a glut of hyperbole, it is fair to say that the Uruguayan striker is a genuine footballing genius. It's just a shame that he makes the headlines too often for the wrong reasons. He has used his hands, his mouth and, yes, his teeth to stain his reputation. That Suárez bit a Chelsea defender during a game in April 2013 didn't come as a massive surprise: he had form in this area. In 2010, while captaining Dutch side Ajax, the player chowed down on an opponent's shoulder, for which he received a seven-match ban. The English FA went further and dished out a 10-game one (only 16 months after giving him an eight-match ban for racial abuse). Every supporter wants their teams' players to show hunger on the pitch, just not that type of appetite.

Over Keane

No look at football's famous sinners is complete without mention of Roy Keane. It's fair to say that the red mist descended upon him a few times. The act of savagery for which he is most notorious is the tackle on Alf-Inge Haaland that all but ended the Norwegian's career. There was plenty of backstory to the knee-high tackle but the challenge itself has had a much longer life span. The Republic of Ireland player initially only received the regulation three-match ban, but mention of the tackle, and in particular its premeditated nature, in his autobiography the following year brought an extra five-match ban and a fine of £150,000. Needless to say, to this day the foul still remains a talking point when discussing the Red Devil legend's career.

Footie Fact

'The Shit Hits the Fan' – newspaper headline after Eric Cantona's infamous attack on a Crystal Palace supporter in 1995.

Off for an early bath

Today it's something of a surprise if a game doesn't feature a flurry of yellow cards and the odd red one. But there was a time when players had to commit something bordering on GBH for the referee to reach into his pocket. There was even a time when there were no cards at all.

Red and yellow cards were invented by referee Ken Aston in the 1960s and were based, in a wonderfully British way, on traffic lights. They were first used at a World Cup in 1970 and in domestic football in 1976. Naturally, players have been setting disciplinary milestones ever since.

First red card: Carlos Caszély, Chile v. West Germany, 1974

First football league red card: David Wagstaffe, Blackburn Rovers v. Leyton Orient, 1976

First England red card at a World Cup: Ray Wilkins, England v. Morocco, 1986

First England red card at Wembley: Paul Scholes, England v. Sweden, 1999

First red card at the new Wembley: Matthew Gill, Exeter v. Morecambe, 2007

First red card in an FA Cup final: Kevin Moran, Manchester United v. Everton, 1985

Quickest red card at a World Cup: 1 minute, José Batista, Uruguay v. Scotland, 1986

First red card in a World Cup final: Pedro Monzón, Argentina v. West Germany, 1990

First red card in the Premier League: Tony Cascarino, Chelsea v. Leeds, 1993

Serious sport has nothing to do with fair play. It is bound up with hatred, jealousy, boastfulness, disregard of all rules and sadistic pleasure in witnessing violence: in other words it is war minus the shooting.

GEORGE ORWELL

THE CELEBRITY
FOOTBALLER

*In 1969, I gave up women and alcohol – it
was the worst 20 minutes of my life.*

GEORGE BEST

Today, the game's top players are automatically thought of as celebrities – there is little if no transition between the two worlds. Sponsorship deals, glossy ads, Sunday newspaper exposés, weddings in *Hello!* magazine – it's the norm not the exception. But there was a time when things were different.

Mr Best, where did it all go wrong?

The celebrity footballer isn't a new concept. Indeed, it's one that goes back further than many may think, before Becks, before Best. Sir Stanley Matthews is often referred to as one of the greatest English players and he can also lay claim to being the first celebrity footballer.

Matthews enjoyed a glittering career at club and national level, but in the era of the maximum wage (no more than £20 a week), his earning power from the game was limited. So, he looked to use his stardom to boost his income: he popped up in films, such as one for the Co-operative Wholesale Society promoting the boots that he endorsed, and adverts, including one for Craven 'A' cigarettes, even though he was a famous non-smoker. He also wasn't a stranger to the front pages. After he retired, he tried his hand at management, including, at the time of apartheid, an all-black team in Soweto. Around the same time, he also very publicly left his wife, going off with a local interpreter he met on a sponsor's tour to Czechoslovakia. He would go on to marry the woman, who was later accused of being a Soviet spy.

Of course, on the infamy scale, it's hard to beat George Best. For all his footballing ability, he is known as much for his appetite for glitz, glamour and women. It all did for him in the end, but he left a canon of anecdotes, quips and quotes. If Matthews entered new territory by lending his name to a few products, then Best all but invaded this new land of opportunity. There were fashion shops, potato snacks, exercise records (with a Miss World, naturally), comics and much, much more. Plus there was the legendary lifestyle, which is summed up rather nicely by an off-the-cuff comment from a bellboy. The bellboy, on delivering champagne to the footballer's hotel room, only to find him in his bed with a scantily clad Miss World, covered in the winnings from a big night at a casino, muttered the words: 'Mr Best, where did it all go wrong?'.

If Matthews was a pioneer and Best a hedonistic explorer, what does that make David Beckham? The all-conquering force? The odd sarong and sex scandal aside, a footballer's celebrity wattage has never shone so bright and so purely. It says something that the clouds that have dimmed this light have been caused by his actions on the field rather than off it. His is a whole different type of footballing celebrity.

Goldenballs, the man with the Midas touch

How do you go about describing the career of David Beckham? There was a time, back in the 1990s, when he was just a young footballer making waves at an up-and-coming Fergie-led Manchester United. But that didn't last long. Before we knew it, he was the centre of the universe. Scoring outlandish goals for fun, marrying one of the world's biggest pop  stars, getting married on purple thrones, wearing sarongs, showing off a new haircut every five minutes, carrying the England team on his shoulders, etc. Everything he did was news.

And little has changed. David Beckham is no longer just a footballer, he's an industry, a universe of his own. He overcame the odds in Spain, he opens football academies across the world, he brought football back to the States, he gave it some James Bond to open the London Olympics, and so on. How long before Her Royal Highness makes him a Sir? Those odds have to be pretty short.

Now he has retired, the question is what will he do? Run a boozer in his home town? Nope. Turn up as a commentator or presenter? Seems unlikely. Get voted in as president of the world? Don't bet against it. This is the level that Becks has taken his football celebrity to. Actually, it is fair to say that the football part hasn't mattered in a while (playing in the US and getting in a few games in Italy and France hardly feels like it counts). He has gone further than any footballer before him: he is now a pure, 24-carat gold celebrity.

David Beckham is the most capped outfield player for England, with 115 appearances for the Three Lions. Only goalkeeper Peter Shilton has more (125).

Tales of the unexpected (and expected)

In an era of such titles as the 'official diesel engine partner of Manchester United' and the 'official coffee, tea and bakery provider of Liverpool FC', it comes as no surprise to see players faces in often silly adverts. While seeing famous footballers advertising airlines in Russia, office equipment in South Korea or mobile phones in Malaysia may look ridiculous, everything is polished, the rough edges all squared away. Perhaps we can blame Gary Lineker and the crisps for that. But there was once a time when a footballer's presence in an advert was both far less common and far less predictable.

Remember George Best? He liked 'birds and booze' as much as football. He wasn't shy of lending his name to a product or two, although many didn't quite match his lifestyle choices. Take his advert for Cookstown sausages – 'Only one thing gets George Best away from football… Cookstown family sausages' went the jingle (really, George?). He also championed the merits of milk (if only it had been a case of the white stuff and not the hard stuff).

Talking of which, Gazza didn't mind using his football fame to feather the nest a bit. His Brut aftershave advert is a peach: fresh from his World Cup 1990 theatrics, a splash or two is enough to get him turning a burly bunch of noisy road workers into a mini urban orchestra. Kevin Keegan, who was one of England's best players before he became one of its poorer managers, also has form when it comes to getting in front of the camera in return for some corporate shilling. His advert for Brut deodorant with British heavyweight boxer Henry Cooper is up there with that volleyball scene in *Top Gun* in terms of unintentionally homoerotic celluloid gold. The two work out furiously together and then join each other for a jolly old time in the shower, telling us how great Brut is.

It's easy to laugh, but at least advertising deodorant or the local pub (yes, really, with Bobby Moore) probably had some credibility with teammates. I'm not sure that can be said for Chicken Tonight (England and Arsenal's Ian Wright, pretending to be posh); Unipart oil filters (the great Pat Jennings of Arsenal and Tottenham, dressed as one while playing in goal); Danepak bacon (Manchester United's Great Dane Peter Schmeichel, singing and playing a range of instruments); or Just for Men hair dye (Portugal legend Luis Figo, faffing with his hair a lot). The money must have been good.

But adverts have proved that footballers aren't all a mercenary bunch, sort of. Kevin Keegan popped up in a 1970s public information film about the Green Cross Code, giving out some sage advice to children, while wearing a pair of incredible flares. Legendary football pundit Jimmy Hill did one around the same time for a motorcycle safety campaign, and a chillingly professional piece of work it was too. Is there a modern equivalent? Well, a while back Pelé did an advert for an erectile dysfunction drug. Does that count?

Footballing adage:
How do you make a small fortune
in football? Start with a big one.

CHAPTER 6

MONEY, MONEY, MONEY

*When I heard my agent repeat the figure of £55,000 [per week],
I nearly swerved off the road. 'He's taking the piss, Jonathan!'
I yelled down the phone. I was trembling with anger.*

ENGLAND DEFENDER ASHLEY COLE, IN HIS AUTOBIOGRAPHY, ON HEARING
A WAGE OFFER FROM THEN EMPLOYERS ARSENAL FC

'They've paid how much!?' is a frequent refrain of the football fan.
No season is complete without a few exuberant transfer fees. But it
wasn't always thus. The concept of the football transfer is nearly as old
as the game itself, but for a few years before player registration was
introduced, they could turn out for any side, whenever they fancied.
If that's unimaginable now, you have to wonder what nineteenth-
century fans would make of the sums swapped for players today.

A tale of two millions

It won't be long before football welcomes its first £100-million player, so before this moment comes to dominate talk of football transfer history, it seems a good time to celebrate the footballer whose transfer was the first to break the £1 million mark.

The first thing to do is give the fanfare to the right player, because a common mistake is to attribute this financial bauble to England's Trevor Francis, who swapped the blue of Birmingham City for the red of Brian Clough's all-conquering Nottingham Forest for £1.1 million in 1979. In fact, the honour belongs to a lesser-known Italian striker by the name of Giuseppe Savoldi.

Savoldi beat Francis to the tape by a good four years when Napoli signed him from Bologna for a world-record fee of two billion lire (£1.2 million) in 1975. However, of the two players, Francis wore his crown with more distinction. While Savoldi maintained a strong scoring record at Napoli and then back at Bologna, he failed to net a regular place in the national team, earning just four caps. In contrast, the English striker can look back on, among others, a European Cup winner's medal, a Super Cup winner's medal and a Coppa Italia winner's medal from his time in Italy, as well as 52 caps for England, including a couple of goals at the 1982 World Cup.

Interestingly, both million-pound men had short stints at Italian club Atalanta in the 1980s, both scoring a single goal in a handful of appearances. However, they never played together, missing each other by a couple of years.

1893   The first three-figure transfer: Willie Groves moves to Aston Villa for £100

1905   Middlesbrough pay £1,000 for Alf Common

1922   Syd Puddefoot leaves West Ham for Falkirk for £5,000

1928   Arsenal pay Bolton £10,890 for the services of David Jack

1961   Luis Suárez is the first six-figure signing; Inter Milan pay £152,000

1975   Giuseppe Savoldi leaves Bologna for Inter Milan for £1.2 million

1979   Trevor Francis is the first British £1-million man, signing for Nottingham Forest

1982   Barcelona break the world transfer record; Maradona signs for £3 million

1985   Napoli break the world transfer record; Maradona signs for £5 million

1996   Newcastle sign Alan Shearer from Southampton for
        £15 million

2000   Luis Figo swaps Barcelona for Real Madrid for £37 million

2001   Zinedine Zidane is signed by Real Madrid for £46.6 million

2001   Gianluigi Buffon is the most expensive goalkeeper of all
        time at £30 million

2002   Rio Ferdinand is the world's most expensive defender at
        £29.1 million

2009   Brazilian Kaká switches from Milan to Real Madrid for
        £56 million

2009   Cristiano Ronaldo leaves Manchester United for Real
        Madrid for £80 million

2011   Chelsea smash the British transfer record: £50 million for
        Liverpool's Fernando Torres

2013   Gareth Bale moves from Tottenham Hotspur to Real Madrid
        for £85.3 million

> ### Footie Fact
>
> Swedish striker Zlatan Ibrahimović is the world's most expensive player by accumulated transfer fees. The total paid to date for his services by the likes of Juventus, Inter Milan, AC Milan, Barcelona and Paris Saint-Germain? A staggering £150.5 million.

Gareth Bale: the €100-million man

The world of football may not have seen the first £100-million player yet, but it has said *hola* to the inaugural €100-million man: Gareth Bale. Spanish giants Real Madrid splashed the unprecedented amount of cash for the next-generation Welsh Wizard in September 2013, continuing its tradition of *galácticos* (world-famous players signed for mammoth fees) and breaking the world transfer record that it had previously set in 2009 on signing Cristiano Ronaldo from Manchester United for £80 million.

So, how did the only Welsh *galáctico* make his way from South Wales to the Santiago Bernabéu? Well, it all began at a Cardiff Civil Service under-nines six-a-side tournament. Bale the boy wonder was spotted by a scout from Southampton, as he glided past opposition players like they weren't there and hammered in or set up goal after goal. This was the moment that would set in motion a journey in which the latest stop is one of the world's greatest football clubs.

His first professional club was the Saints on the south coast, where the winger started out as a left back, at the tender age of 16. Just over a year after becoming the second youngest player to turn out for Southampton, during which time he became known more for his creativity and free-kick taking than his defending, he was signed by Tottenham Hotspur. It was at White Hart Lane that his career truly took off, although it wasn't all plain sailing. His first few seasons were interrupted by injury and it wasn't until the 2011–12 season that this star began to really shine, helping Spurs progress in the Champion's League and picking up the PFA Young Player of the Year Award.

From there on in, the eyes of the world's media were firmly fixed on Bale as he began to dominate games in the way only great players do. Goals and awards flowed, before the men from Madrid arrived with an offer he and Spurs couldn't resist.

Footie Fact

There was a time when a footballer's wage was so small that players had to have a job outside the game. The story goes that 1940s and 1950s England legend Sir Tom Finney would turn up to a home game with his plumbing tools in a wheelbarrow, and once he was done terrorising the opposition's defence, he'd pick them up again and head off to finish the job. Not something you'd find Lionel Messi doing today.

Real Madrid's other galácticos

Real Madrid is famous for its *galácticos*. The club may have eased up a little on its outlay of late, but the talent that has put on the famous white shirt has been truly incredible. Here is a pick of the best and most influential of recent times.

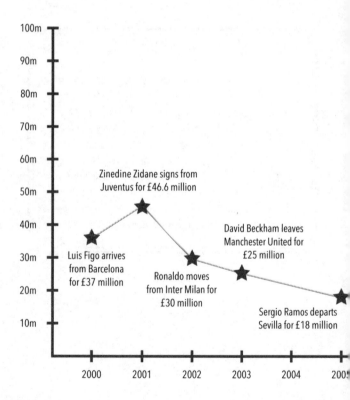

Zinedine Zidane signs from Juventus for £46.6 million

Luis Figo arrives from Barcelona for £37 million

Ronaldo moves from Inter Milan for £30 million

David Beckham leaves Manchester United for £25 million

Sergio Ramos departs Sevilla for £18 million

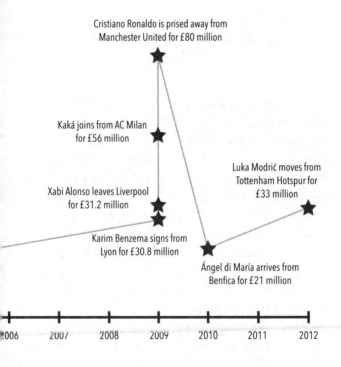

Cristiano Ronaldo is prised away from
Manchester United for £80 million

Kaká joins from AC Milan
for £56 million

Luka Modrić moves from
Tottenham Hotspur for
£33 million

Xabi Alonso leaves Liverpool
for £31.2 million

Karim Benzema signs from
Lyon for £30.8 million

Ángel di María arrives from
Benfica for £21 million

2006 2007 2008 2009 2010 2011 2012

THE JOY OF
FOOTBALL GROUNDS

*Wembley is the cathedral of football. It is the capital
of football and it is the heart of football.*

PELÉ

When it comes to the joy of football, part of it is to be found in the
stadia where the game is actually played. Going to watch your team
play, stepping inside the stadium and becoming part of something
bigger: there's a reverence to it, a bristling sense of anticipation, an
electricity to the events that connects you in a completely different
way to watching on television.

And then there's playing in a stadium. As a kid kicking a ball
around a park, with makeshift goalposts and the pitch as wide as the
patch of grass you're playing on, and even as an adult toiling away on
potato fields or boggy hillsides at the weekends for an amateur side,
you dream of playing at a proper football ground, with its terraces,
floodlights and groundkeepers.

Not that every stadium is the same, far from it. The charm is
that visiting each one a unique experience, even in this age of the
identikit ground.

The Wembley way

The greatest stadium in English football is undoubtedly Wembley. It is a ground that is steeped in history and inspires awe not just nationally but across the world. Part of the mystique that surrounds and defines Wembley is that to play there is an achievement in itself. To see your team walk out on to the famous pitch means that they are taking part in a showpiece game, whether a semi-final or a final; they've fought hard to get there. A game here holds with it the chance of glory.

Wembley is also the home of the England football team and there are few football-obsessed English kids that won't have imagined themselves lining up before the game, belting out the national anthem and going on to score the winning goal. To play for England, or whatever your national side may be, is what every young player thinks about when they pull the shirt, shorts and socks on for the first time. And if you're English, this dream is irrevocably linked to Wembley.

Of course, there are two Wembley stadiums these days. The original, completed just days before it hosted its first FA Cup final and initially known as the Empire Stadium, was built for a country whose belief in its status in the world was unshakeable. Football was no different and Wembley with its famous Twin Towers was a monument to England's lofty position in the game.

Of course, to borrow a phrase from Sir Alex Ferguson, English football was knocked off its perch, but Wembley remained hallowed turf up until the decision was made to rebuild it from scratch. If the new Wembley doesn't have the same soul, it is no less imposing. The second largest stadium in Europe, with its roof and arch visible across London, it is very much a modern wonder.

Wembley milestones

1923 — The original Wembley Stadium hosts its first FA Cup final between Bolton Wanderers and West Ham

1924 — The first international game is played at Wembley, England draw 1-1 with Scotland

1948 — The stadium plays host to the 1948 Olympic Games

1951 — The first England international match at Wembley not involving Scotland takes place. Argentina are beaten 2-1

1963 — Wembley welcomes the European Cup final for the first time as AC Milan overcome Benfica 2-1

1966 — Wembley is the venue for the World Cup final as England defeat West Germany in extra time to lift the greatest prize in football

1968 — Wembley hosts its second European Cup Final, with Manchester United becoming the first English winners

1996	England hosts Euro 96 and the final at Wembley sees Germany win 2-1 against the Czech Republic, with a golden goal in extra time
2000	The last FA Cup final at the old Wembley takes place: Chelsea beat Aston Villa 1-0
2000	The old Wembley sees its last England international, with the Three Lions losing 1-0 to old foes Germany
2007	The first competitive game is held at the new Wembley: Stevenage Borough beat Kidderminster Harriers in the non-league FA Trophy
2007	The first England international takes place at the new Wembley: England draw 1-1 with Brazil
2011	The new Wembley hosts its first Champions League final: Barcelona defeat Manchester United 3-1
2013	Borussia Dortmund and Bayern Munich contest the second Champions League final at the new Wembley, celebrating 150 years of the FA

Football grounds: the unusual and the unbelievable

Every supporter has their own theatre of dreams. From the Camp Nou in Spain where thousands regularly come to worship Barcelona to the Maracanã in Brazil that embodies the style and history of *jogo bonito*. Whether they're old grounds whose rough edges and rudimentary structures are testament to another era or sparkling new stadiums that are symbols of a hopeful future, they are all cathedrals of football. And they are all different. Although some are more different than others.

Every stadium has its quirks, whether major or minor.

Until recently, when you visited AFC Bournemouth, you'd find a ground with only three sides – the fourth was open, with the trees that lined that end offering those willing to climb the chance of watching for free.

Go to Brisbane Road, home of Leyton Orient, and at each corner you'll see a block of flats, whose terraces almost protrude into play.

Head to the ground of Luton Town to support your team and to get into the away end you have to enter through some terraced houses.

Of course, it isn't just British grounds that are unusual. It's a worldwide phenomenon.

Perhaps one of the most striking football grounds in the world is the home of Portuguese team Braga. The stadium was built in a quarry, seemingly squeezed in between giant slabs of rock. There is seating on only two sides, with one end a craggy cliff face and the other offering views of the city below. Its relative newness – it was constructed for the 2004 European Championship – only adds to the sense of marvellous oddity.

From one rock formation to another: the Omnilife stadium in Guadalajara, Mexico, soars out of the earth like an erupting volcano, with its white roof the ring of smoke hanging above the crater. The local landscape was the inspiration behind this incredible stadium.

The Janguito Malucelli stadium in Brazil takes the link with nature even further. It is the country's first eco-friendly football ground: there is no hard metal seating, just seats embedded in the grassy hillside, and reclaimed wood is used throughout with no concrete in sight.

If you played football in your back garden as a kid, chances are that you had to pay regular visits to your neighbours' gardens, officially or surreptitiously, to retrieve your ball. Scrambling over a fence or two was part of the fun. So imagine playing at the Vesturi á Eiðinum in Vagur in the Faroe Islands. As close to the rugged coastline as you can get without toppling into the water, the stadium employs people in boats to fetch wayward shots.

From by the water to on it: that's where the multi-purpose Marina Bay Float Stadium in Singapore can be found. As its name suggests, this football pitch has actually been built on the water, which in this case is the Marina Reservoir. The world's largest floating stage, with fan seating for up to 30,000 positioned just back from the waterside, the platform is made entirely of steel and can take the weight of up to 9,000 people. Which is plenty for a game of football.

Football stadiums by seating capacity
(including stadiums used for other sports alongside football)

Rungnado May Day Stadium
150,000
Pyongyang
North Korea

Salt Lake Stadium
120,000
Kolkata
India

Camp Nou
99,354
Barcelona
Spain

FNB Stadium
94,713
Johannesburg
South Africa

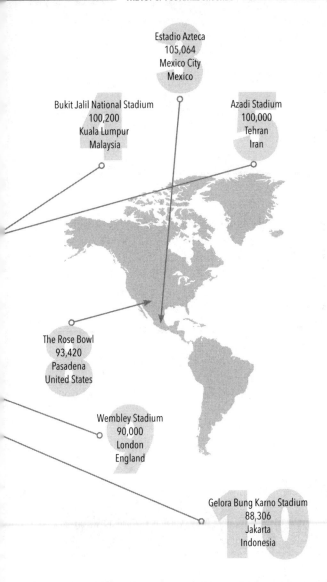

Estadio Azteca
105,064
Mexico City
Mexico

Bukit Jalil National Stadium
100,200
Kuala Lumpur
Malaysia

Azadi Stadium
100,000
Tehran
Iran

The Rose Bowl
93,420
Pasadena
United States

Wembley Stadium
90,000
London
England

Gelora Bung Karno Stadium
88,306
Jakarta
Indonesia

Footie Fact

The highest ever attendance at a football stadium? Some reports say that over 200,000 people were in the crowd for the first FA Cup Final at Wembley in 1923. A similar number is thought to have crammed into the Centenario stadium in Uruguay to watch the 1950 World Cup final between Uruguay and Brazil.

CHAPTER 8

MANAGERS: THE BEST AND THE WORST

Rome wasn't built in a day but I wasn't on that particular job.
BRIAN CLOUGH

Football's heroes and villains aren't just found on the pitch. They're in the dugouts too. Worshipped or vilified, there is no shortage of theatre: a manager is either the master puppeteer who guides his team to glory or the inept meddler who is the cause of his side's failure. Over the length of a career, a manager can regularly switch identities. The eccentric, the egotistical, the enigmatic, those at the end of their tethers: there's never a dull moment.

The best bosses in the business

How do you choose the game's best managers? How do you judge success? By the amount of silverware in the trophy room? By keeping an unfancied side playing in the top league? By reinventing the way a team plays and creating a whole new footballing philosophy? And then there's your own club bias. Fortunately some managers are just so good that none of this matters.

Pep: the master of tika-taka

The world of football management has seen some iconic figures, but at present few wield a greater aura than Spain's Pep Guardiola: the legendary Barcelona midfielder who became the club's even more legendary manager, before taking up the hot seat at German *übermannschaft* Bayern Munich.

Guardiola transformed Barcelona and made *tika-taka* (a style based on short passes, movement and maintaining possession) into a football phenomenon. In his first season alone, he won the unprecedented Spanish Treble of La Liga, the Copa del Rey and the Champions League. Over the course of four seasons, he collected a staggering 14 trophies, including an amazing six pieces of silverware within the 2009 calendar year, adding the Spanish Supercopa, the UEFA Super Cup and the FIFA Club World Cup to an already historic haul. He nearly repeated the trick in 2011, only missing out on the Copa del Rey.

Some thought he might struggle to successfully blend German steel with his Iberian *tika-taka* at Bayern. It didn't take him long to prove his doubters wrong – very wrong.

Jürgen the German

How can you be a manager of a team other than Bayern Munich in the German Bundesliga and be considered one of the best in the world? By being Jürgen Klopp, that's how. His reign at Borussia Dortmund, and the success that it has brought, is emblematic of how a change in philosophy has transformed German football over the past decade.

He turned up at Borussia Dortmund with the club languishing in mid-table and instantly got results: the side won the German Supercup in his first season. Thereafter he showed that other teams could be as good as perennial champions Bayern Munich. He showed that they could be even better. Dortmund won the Bundesliga championship for the first time in a decade under Klopp in 2011; then they claimed it again in 2012, all the time playing with a style based on youth, attack and confidence.

Bayern Munich may be back to their formidable best with Pep Guardiola pulling the strings, but Borussia Dortmund are still a force to be reckoned with thanks to Klopp.

The Special One

Or should that be 'the Happy One'? José Mourinho may have rechristened himself during his second stint at Chelsea, but his managerial career, which has spanned Porto, Chelsea, Inter Milan and Real Madrid, is without a doubt very special. Love him or hate him, he is one of the best managers in the business.

So, where do you start with Mourinho? With the fact that he earned his managerial spurs under the late Sir Bobby Robson at Barcelona? That he guided Portuguese side Porto to Champions League glory? That he turned Chelsea into a dominant force in the English Premier League and Europe? That he won six trophies, including the Italian Treble in 2009–10, in his three years at Inter Milan? That he won La Liga, Copa del Rey and Supercopa titles with Real Madrid in Spain despite playing against Guardiola's Barcelona? Or with his UEFA Manager of the Year award in 2003 and 2004? Or his FIFA World Coach of the Year award in 2010? Or his nine-year, 150-match, four-club unbeaten home-league record?

And then there are the accolades he has picked up outside the game: *New Statesman* Man of the Year and Spanish *Rolling Stone* Rockstar of the Year, as well as his own children's cartoon in Portugal called *Mourinho and the Special Ones*. Wherever he goes, he wins. Chelsea must be happy to have him back.

The Governor from Govan

Manchester United's dip in form since Sir Alex Ferguson retired only illustrates just how great a manager the Governor from Govan was. He helmed the club for almost 30 years, a length of time that is simply incredible, and achieved a level of success that puts him in the company of British managerial greats, such as Matt Busby, Bill Shankly and Bob Paisley.

Much is made of the time Ferguson was allowed at Manchester United to nurture a winning team and the fact that any modern manager wouldn't be permitted such grace. However, the Scot had already made his managerial mark and had achieved one of his greatest triumphs. Before he turned up at Old Trafford, Ferguson was manager of Scottish team Aberdeen, where he managed to wrestle the domestic league title away from the clutches of the mighty Celtic-Rangers axis, but, more importantly, he steered his side to European glory.

In 1982–83, Ferguson led Aberdeen, a relatively small Scottish club, to a European Cup Winners' Cup final, beating the likes of Bayern Munich and Tottenham Hotspur along the way. Spanish giants Real Madrid were the opposition in the showpiece game and few outside Aberdeen expected them to win. But they did, 2–1, becoming only the third Scottish team to claim a European trophy. They went on to defeat European Cup champions Hamburg in the UEFA Super Cup too.

Ferguson's ability didn't go unnoticed and he went on to manage the Scottish national team at the 1986 World Cup before job offers in the top league in England started to pour in. Reportedly turning down the likes of Glasgow Rangers, Arsenal, Spurs and Wolverhampton Wanderers, he eventually said yes to Manchester United. The rest, as they say, is history.

Twenty-six years later, on hanging up his famous hairdryer, he could look back on an Old Trafford dynasty that not only included many great teams, but featured players such as David Beckham, Paul Scholes, Roy Keane, Eric Cantona, Ryan Giggs, Cristiano Ronaldo and Wayne Rooney, and that won 13 Premier League titles, five FA Cups, four League Cups, two Champions Leagues, one UEFA Super Cup and one FIFA Club World Cup.

Footie Fact

No English manager has ever led a team to the English Premier League title. Howard Wilkinson was the last Englishman to steer a club to top-flight victory, with Leeds United in 1992, the year before the Premier League was launched.

Footie Fact

Which English team has had the most managers in one season? Manchester City in 1995–96 takes some beating. The club appointed three full-time managers and two caretaker managers over the course of the season. They were relegated.

REPORTER: *So, Gordon, in what areas do you think Middlesbrough were better than you today?*

GORDON STRACHAN: *Mainly that big green one out there.*

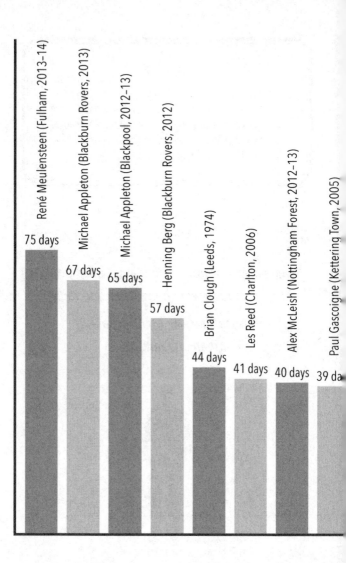

- 75 days — René Meulensteen (Fulham, 2013–14)
- 67 days — Michael Appleton (Blackburn Rovers, 2013)
- 65 days — Michael Appleton (Blackpool, 2012–13)
- 57 days — Henning Berg (Blackburn Rovers, 2012)
- 44 days — Brian Clough (Leeds, 1974)
- 41 days — Les Reed (Charlton, 2006)
- 40 days — Alex McLeish (Nottingham Forest, 2012–13)
- 39 da — Paul Gascoigne (Kettering Town, 2005)

Welcome to the club and goodbye

For all the great, lengthy managerial reigns in football, there are also those that were painfully short. Whether through incompetence, impatience or ill fortune, the English game boasts many examples of managers for whom getting their feet under the table proved a distant, unachievable dream.

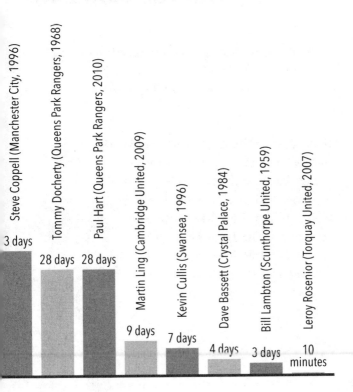

CHAPTER 9

THE FAMOUS AND
THE FOOTBALLING

*Every fan you ask will say he wants to see lively, open football,
but what the fan really wants to see is his team win.*
FORMER ARSENAL CHAIRMAN DENIS HILL-WOOD

Seeing a famous fan in the crowd is a strangely
illuminating moment. It's like you've been let into
a secret. And the sense of wonder is amplified if
the relationship is an odd one. Why does Prince
William support Aston Villa? How come
Cameron Diaz is listed as a fan of Brentford?
And what is Mikhail Gorbachev doing
following Wigan Athletic? It just makes the
beautiful game even more fascinating.

A royal seal of approval

Why the second in line to the throne is an Aston Villa fan is something of a mystery, but it does mean we can write 'Prince William is a Villain' (it's the club's nickname) without fear of being locked up in the Tower of London. Apparently he has supported the Birmingham-based team since he was young and was given to donning Villa socks for games at Eton (it's not often that Aston Villa and Eton are mentioned in the same sentence). Now, as president of the FA, he has ample opportunity to watch games, although his beloved team are, alas, rarely to be seen in showpiece matches.

The reported choices of his brother and grandmother seem more appropriate: Prince Harry and the Queen are both said to support Arsenal. The geography makes sense – the Gunners are from London – and the club's status as one of football's aristocrats also fits the bill. Maybe William was inspired by his dad: Prince Charles is a confirmed fan of Burnley, which, like Aston Villa, play in claret and blue and whose best days, at the moment at least, lie firmly in the past.

From one stage to another

Actors' choice of football teams can be just as leftfield. Aside from Cameron Diaz's love for the Bees, Tom Hanks is rather unfathomably another famous Aston Villa fan, while how Tom Cruise came to follow Arsenal is something of a head-scratcher. Of course, some affiliations, whether fleeting or diehard, make perfect sense: Hackney-born Ray Winstone is a big West Ham fan, Catherine Zeta-Jones supports Swansea City, the place of her birth, and Sean Bean, heroic in *Game of Thrones* and villainous in *Goldeneye,* and a son of Sheffield, calls Sheffield United his team.

From a 007 baddie to the man, or men, himself: James Bond has several teams, or at least the actors who have played him do. Daniel Craig, the spy's latest incarnation, is a supporter of a global heavyweight with a grand heritage, much like the character, in Liverpool, while Timothy Dalton's allegiance is less conventional, much like his spin on the world's favourite spook, with his side being Derby County. Original big-screen Bond Sean Connery is true to his Scottish roots in his support of Glasgow Rangers.

The politics of the game

Politicians are football fans too. It can be hard to marry the two worlds, but they have quite a lot in common. For a start, football supporters and MPs enjoy bellowing at the opposition on a regular basis (with its two opposing stands, the House of Commons is almost set up like a football ground) and there is a tribalism about how both act: most invest in a lifelong loyalty to one set of colours and take up views accordingly. Furthermore, football and politics both take the summer off except in extraordinary circumstances.

As with other spheres of famous fandom, politics throws up some interesting allegiances. Former Labour leader Michael Foot was a passionate Plymouth Argyle supporter, so much so that the club made him an honorary player and presented him with a shirt featuring the squad number 90 on his 90th birthday. More recent Labour men, and prime ministers, Tony Blair and Gordon Brown put their support of Newcastle United and Raith Rovers on record. To add some balance, former Conservative No.10 resident John Major is a lifelong Chelsea fan, and David Cameron is apparently an Aston Villa man, an allegiance that is presumably owed to the fact that his uncle used to be chairman of the club.

Moving into Europe, it shouldn't come as a surprise that former Italian Prime Minister Silvio Berlusconi is a big AC Milan fan because he owns the club. However, the supposed choice of German Chancellor Angela Merkel is more surprising – she is an honorary member of East German team Energie Cottbus, which currently reside in the second tier of German football. French President François Hollande is reportedly a fan of AS Monaco. As for why Mikhail Gorbachev is associated with the Latics (Wigan Athletic), it may have something to do with a visit he is said to have made to the team's ground when he was secretary of Soviet football side Metalist Kharkiv. The fates of Gorbachev and the club remained closely linked: the secretary went on to become the last President of the Soviet Union and as a result Metalist went on to become a Ukrainian team.

Singing their praises

The world of music is seemingly a more natural partner for football than aristocracy or politics, and there are plenty of musicians who sing their allegiances from the rooftops. Of course, among this chorus of fandom, there is the occasional off-key harmony.

 Michael Jackson – Exeter City

 Robbie Williams – Port Vale

 Fatboy Slim – Brighton & Hove Albion

 Sir Elton John – Watford

 Ozzy Osbourne – Aston Villa

 Bob Marley – Tottenham Hotspur

 Suggs – Chelsea

 Bill Wyman – Crystal Palace

 Paul McCartney – Everton

Ian Brown – Manchester United

 Robert Plant – Wolverhampton Wanderers

 Rod Stewart – Celtic

 Luciano Pavarotti – AS Roma

 Plácido Domingo – Barcelona

 Roger Daltrey – Arsenal

 Sting – Newcastle

 Dr Dre – Liverpool

 Snoop Dogg (aka Snoop Lion) – Barcelona

 Jarvis Cocker – Sheffield Wednesday

 Pete Doherty – Queens Park Rangers

 Slash – Stoke City

Finding the right pitch

While celebrity football fans are to be found far and wide, a celebrity football player – not a musician or an actor who pulls on the boots for the occasional charity game, but someone who has actually played professionally – is a much rarer beast altogether.

A recent recruit to this very select club is Louis Tomlinson, a member of British boy band One Direction, although his credentials aren't quite bona fide. The Doncaster-born pop star may have turned out for his home town's reserve side, but his appearance has as much to do with raising money for charity and for the financially stricken club as it does with his footballing skills.

Spanish crooner Julio Iglesias, a pin-up from a completely differently era, did things the other way round: he swapped belting a ball for belting out a melody. Better known as father of Enrique these

days, Iglesias Senior was a mega star in his own right and before he took over the world of pop, he played in goal for the Real Madrid reserve team. Reportedly quite the player, he only hung up his gloves following a car accident.

While Tomlinson and Iglesias can both claim to have played professionally, there are a number of celebrities for whom such status was just out of reach despite their best efforts. Matt Smith may never have become the 11th Doctor in Doctor Who if injury hadn't called time on a playing career that included Leicester City, Northampton Town and Nottingham Forest youth teams, while perennial rocker Rod Stewart and celebrity chef Gordon Ramsay had trials for Celtic and Rangers respectively.

Game changers

Playing two top sports professionally at the same time is all but impossible these days, such is the commitment that making the grade within one requires. Go back to the first half of the twentieth century and you'll find plenty of examples of footballers-cum-cricketers-cum-rugby players turning out in multiple sports for local and national sides. Famous examples includes William Foulke, a 24 stone, 6 ft 4 in Shropshire lad who captained Chelsea and appeared for England, as well as playing first-class cricket for Derbyshire; and Denis Compton, an FA Cup and League title winner with Arsenal and an all-rounder with Middlesex County Cricket Club and England.

All of this makes the case of Ian Botham even more incredible. His legendary cricketing exploits require little explanation, but to say he is regarded as England's greatest all-rounder, however his lesser-known footballing career certainly does. While he was batting and bowling for England and Somerset in the 1980s, he also made a handful of appearances for Yeovil Town and Scunthorpe United. He scored just one goal in nearly 30 appearances, hitting the back of the net in a game for the Somerset-based Glovers.

Footie Fact

The Nevilles of Manchester have to be one of the UK's most successful sporting families. Brothers Gary and Phil played for Manchester United and England, winning countless trophies for the former, while sister Tracey, twin of Phil, represented England at netball, appearing at the 1998 and 2002 Commonwealth Games.

CHAPTER 10

ALL THE KIT

The players couldn't pick each other out.

SIR ALEX FERGUSON DEFLECTS THE BLAME FOR MANCHESTER UNITED'S SURPRISING DEFEAT AGAINST SOUTHAMPTON IN 1996 BY POINTING THE FINGER AT THE SIDE'S NEW, AND NOW INFAMOUS, GREY KIT. HE ORDERED THE PLAYERS TO CHANGE INTO DIFFERENT SHIRTS AT HALF TIME. THEY STILL LOST.

Playing football today requires a bag full of kit. Socks, shorts and a shirt are just the start. There's a decision to make about what type of football boots you'll need – long studs, short studs, moulded or AstroTurf boots? – and it'll be wise not to forget your shin pads and some tape to keep them in place. If you're playing in winter, you might want to include some under-armour, gloves and a woolly hat, as well as some Deep Heat. Not to mention a tracksuit to warm up in and, if you're going to be really professional about it, some hand warmers for your pockets. Back when the game as we know it was in its infancy, things were a lot simpler.

Knickers not shorts

When organised football first became a staple of British life in the late nineteenth century, players took to the pitch, not in high-tech kits designed to aid mobility and endurance, adorned with the numbers and names of players and sponsors' logos, but in something more rudimentary altogether. For a start, you didn't wear shorts – it was knickerbockers or long trousers, whose baggy material was often secured with braces or a belt. And there was no deliberating over which pair of fluorescent lightweight boots you were going to put on – footballers in this era played in their everyday shoes or work boots, which were invariably heavy and became even more so in the wet. The height of technology and ingenuity in these days was to nail some leather to your footwear to improve the grip (unsurprisingly it didn't take long for this practice to be outlawed, as flinging your feet around with nails potentially protruding from your boots can't have been the safest).

Talking of safety, it took a while for shin pads to be worn on the football field. Before that you just had to man up and take any blows received, intentional or otherwise. The first shin pads were fashioned out of a cut-down pair of cricket pads and the idea caught on fairly quickly. It would be a while before the shin pad as we know it today was invented and, as football shifted from being the pursuit of the wealthy amateur to the game of the working class around the turn of the twentieth century, financial restrictions led to some novel ways of replicating the bastardised cricket pad, most notably the stuffing of old copies of *Reader's Digest* or any other suitably thick magazine down the front of socks.

Around the same time, as the game became professionalised and more rules were introduced, the concept of boots specifically for football emerged. Made of leather, they were still heavy and rose up above the ankle like modern-day rugby boots. Many also had hard toecaps (presumably, as the balls were equally dense in those days, the extra sturdiness allowed great power and not for any malicious reasons) and you could have any colour as long as it was black.

It wasn't until the 1950s that boots as we know them today, shaped below the ankle, were first introduced. Now, of course, boots look very different: professional and amateur footballers strap on footwear of every perceivable colour – the more lurid the better seems to be the norm – and have them personalised with their initials, shirt numbers or even kids' names. How things have changed.

On the subject of specialised kit, it took over 40 years for goalkeepers to be officially required to wear a shirt that differentiated them from their teammates. That's not to say some effort was made prior to the ruling in 1909: goalkeepers often wore woolly jumpers to set themselves apart from colleagues who did their best to wear tops that indicated they were on the same side. As for gloves, these didn't become a regular piece of kit for goalkeepers until the 1970s, so those hard, heavy balls had to be stopped with bare hands alone.

Getting shirty

Today, every professional football team has at least three strips – a home, an away and a third kit (should the away kit also clash with opponents' colours) – and these are changed every couple of years. Every team has its distinctive colour, but has alternatives to avoid clashing with opponents. Back in Victorian England, kits were a lot less sophisticated; indeed, it took a while for the idea of any type of kit to catch on. Initially players would wear what they could get their hands on and the only indication of what team they played for was a coloured cap or sash.

However, it didn't take too long for standard strips to emerge and the early kits were quite lurid as clubs embraced links to schools, universities and other sporting organisations. As the game became democratised and clubs rather than individuals became responsible for supplying kits, this trend changed, with basic colours fast becoming the norm. Around this time, shorts began to be worn rather than knickerbockers or trousers, although they were still referred to as 'knickers'.

Shirt numbering was introduced in the 1930s but, this development aside, football shirts didn't really change much until the 1970s, when clubs pursued individualism with more purpose and started selling replica strips. The decade also saw the advent of shirt sponsorship, although only initially in Europe. German football was an early adopter of shirt sponsorship and in 1973 Eintracht Braunschweig is credited with being the first team to don a sponsor's logo, which somewhat controversially belonged to Jägermeister. The herbal liqueur maker's relationship with the side continued until the late 1980s and included an attempt by the company to get the team renamed Eintracht Jägermeister. However, the German FA wasn't having any of it.

The English FA was far less progressive than most of its continental peers and it rigidly imposed a ban on shirt sponsorship until 1977 when Derby signed a deal with Saab, albeit wearing the logoed tops only once. Liverpool were the first team to wear a shirt featuring a sponsor in a league match – the players' tops had Hitachi emblazoned across them in 1978. Non-league team Kettering Town tried to copy what had been going on for several years in Europe and earn some money from shirt sponsorship in 1976: the side ran out once with Kettering Tyres on their chests, but the FA clamped down on it swiftly with the threat of a fine way beyond the means of such a small club. Kettering backed down, but their place in history was secure.

Today, companies pay millions of pounds for their names to be placed on the right shirts: in 2013, Real Madrid signed a shirt sponsorship deal with Emirates worth £32 million per year for five seasons; while Barcelona's deal to wear the name of the Qatar Foundation on their shirts is said to be worth £25 million annually. Liverpool (Standard Chartered), Man City (Etihad) and Manchester United (Chevrolet) all have shirt deals estimated at around £20 million a year. It's a long way from Kettering Tyres.

Cameroon and the rise and fall of the football onesie

Football shirts, or at least some of them, have long been considered fashion items, whether good or bad. The football pitch or ground is no longer the only preserve of a football shirt and the market for classic replica tops has exploded in recent years. Indeed, there is an example of football getting the jump on the fashion industry. Yes, the onesie was on the football pitch long before it was on the high street. But the innovation from Cameroon (and Puma) didn't last long.

The Cameroon onesie, or skintight leotard depending on how you see it, made its debut in 2004 at the African Nations Cup. Why? Well, perhaps it had something to do with the heat, or maybe it was all in the name of pure innovation? Whatever the reason, FIFA took the utmost umbrage and told the Indomitable Lions to bin the new kits, citing a rule about having separate shorts and shirts. Rather surprisingly (or not as the team had got into hot water over short-lived sleeveless tops in 2002), Cameroon stood their ground and played on in the man-sized Babygros. Not that it did them any good: FIFA docked the side six points from its 2006 World Cup qualifying campaign and hit it with a big fine. Puma rather cheekily coughed up the money and Cameroon relented, as did FIFA eventually, restoring the points on appeal, and that was the end of the football onesie.

Footie Fact

Football has seen its fair share of unusual kit fads, from nasal strips and large dollops of Vaseline on the front of shirts that some think improve air intake, to Alice bands that keep long hair out of the eyes and snoods for cold Wednesday nights in Stoke. The latest innovation? Kinesio tape from Japan that supposedly gives players an edge by helping to mend injuries.

CHAPTER 11

EUROPEAN CLUB FOOTBALL

*Playing football is very simple, but playing simple
football is the hardest thing there is.*

DUTCH FOOTBALL LEGEND JOHAN CRUYFF

When it comes to bragging rights, what makes one club team better than another? If we're talking about the top sides, it's who's done best in Europe. Yes, league championships are important and domestic cups look nice in the trophy cabinet, but European success is the ultimate benchmark – and the very best European cup to win (there have been a few over the years) is the UEFA Champions League.

A history of European cup football

1955 – The European Champions Cup, or European Cup, is established

1955 – João Baptista Martins of Portuguese side
Sporting Lisbon scores the first European Cup goal

1956 – The first European Cup is won by Real Madrid

1960 – The European Cup Winners' Cup is launched, contested by
the winners of all European domestic cups

1961 – Fiorentina are the first team to
win the European Cup Winners' Cup

1967 – Celtic become the first British team
to win the European Cup

1968 – Manchester United
are the first English side to
claim the European Cup

1971 – The UEFA Cup is held for
the first time; teams qualify based
on their performance in domestic league and cup competitions

1972 –Tottenham Hotspur are the victors
in the inaugural UEFA Cup final

1985 – Juventus become the first club to win all
three European cups

1986 – Romanians Steaua Bucureşti are the first Eastern
European side to win the European Cup

1992 – The UEFA Champions League replaces
the European Cup

1993 – French side Marseille win the
first Champions League trophy

1998 – The Champions League
format is expanded to include
the best runners up

1999 – Manchester United are the first
British winners of the Champions League

1999 – The European Cup Winners'
Cup is retired by UEFA. Italian team
Lazio are the last winners

2005 – 50 years of the European Cup/Champions League:
Liverpool are the winners, claiming their fifth trophy

2009 – The UEFA Cup is expanded and rechristened
the UEFA Europa League

2010 – Spain's Atlético Madrid are the first
UEFA Europa League champions

The Champions League era

1992 was full of monumental moments in European football. The Premier League, or Premiership as it was initially known, was launched, and England crashed out of Euro 92 in Sweden without a single point; but perhaps the most significant was the decision by UEFA to take its premier European cup competition and go back to the drawing board.

Out went the European Cup, with Red Star Belgrade of Yugoslavia the last side, and only the second from Eastern Europe, to claim the trophy. On a May night in Bari, Italy, a trophy that was soon to be consigned to history was claimed by a team from a country that would suffer the same fate. The replacement was the Champions League, featuring, as it name suggested, a new league format to replace the old purely knockout system. The competition has gone from strength to strength and has become more of a spectacle than its predecessor ever was.

What makes Champions League nights so special? Well, a good place to start is the players. Once upon a time, the only way fans watched footballers from different continents was at the World Cup. OK, a handful of stars from places as exotic as Brazil or Argentina, or even Poland or Russia, made it to top European clubs, but that was about it. The Champions League changed the picture, its growth, both physical and financial, driving the globalisation of the game. Today the Champions League isn't just the place to see the best European players, it's where you can watch the cream of the world's footballing talent. That's a big change. Not that watching a league game on a wet January night in Stoke can't be rewarding; it's just knowing that you can also tune in to Barcelona or Bayern Munich taking on Paris Saint-Germain or Juventus, and see Argentina's Lionel Messi, Cameroon's Samuel Eto'o, Uruguay's Edinson Cavani or the Ivory Coast's Didier Drogba strut their stuff, makes football more special. Football before the Champions League really was a different world.

It's not just the big teams and big players that are now more readily consumable to fans. It might not be fashionable to say it, but the Champions League, and the decision to expand the format to include the best runners up as well as the domestic league champions, has introduced fans to a lot more teams in Europe. Before 1992, little was known about teams from less glamorous leagues; there was a passing interest if your team was playing them, but that was all, and chances were that these sides were knocked out of the competition pretty early. OK, the vast sums of money available to the traditional heavyweights still means that it's the big clubs that end up at the business end of things, but new and less fancied teams are elbowing their way into the picture, and for the fan who craves all things football, to have this access is incredible, even if occasionally your team finds itself on the wrong side of an upset.

Footie Fact

There is only one manager who has won the UEFA Champions League, the World Cup and the European Championship: Vicente del Bosque. He took Real Madrid to Champions League victory in 2000 and 2002, and won the World Cup and the European Championship with Spain in 2010 and 2012 respectively.

Europe's best

It's a natural desire, almost a subconscious act, for the football fan: wanting to know who's the best in Europe, whether it's a player, a manager or a team. It's a debate that can fill a whole evening and still end in disagreement. It's a devil's advocate's dream of ifs, buts and maybes. How do you decide? Well, it makes sense to start with some ground rules.

Want to know who are Europe's best? Well, let's focus solely on the top competition, the Champions League, and let's consider achievements in the new competition on the same merits as those in the old European Cup. So, who is the best team? If we're talking trophy wins, that simple: it's Spanish giants Real Madrid, winners on nine occasions before the 2013–14 competition, including a run of five consecutive triumphs between 1956 and 1960. The team closest to challenging the record of Los Blancos is AC Milan from Italy, victors on seven occasions. As for English teams, Liverpool have won it five times, Manchester United three times and Nottingham Forest twice (which were back-to-back victories in 1979 and 1980), while Chelsea and Aston Villa have got their hands on it once.

How about managers? The most successful manager in the competition is Liverpool's Bob Paisley who won the European Cup in 1977, 1978 and 1981. However, Pep Guardiola, José Mourinho or Carlo Ancelotti can equal the record if they steer a club to the trophy again, and given the clubs they are in charge of and the players and budgets at their disposal, you wouldn't bet against them doing so.

So that leaves the players. Who has won the most trophies? One player stands alone on six wins: Real Madrid's Francisco Gento, who picked up winners' medals for the Spanish side between 1956 and 1960 and in 1966. As for modern-day players, Paolo Maldini can look back at five wins for AC Milan, with the last one coming 18 years after the first, while Clarence Seedorf and Samuel Eto'o have four triumphs to their names, with the former the only man in the competition's history to win the trophy with three different teams (Ajax, Real Madrid and AC Milan). The most successful English player? Step forward Liverpool defender Phil Neal with four wins in 1977, 1978, 1981 and 1984.

Footie Fact

The last British manager to win the UEFA Champions League was Sir Alex Ferguson, who led Manchester United to victories in 1999 and 2008. Before that it was Liverpool boss Joe Fagan in 1984.

SCREEN ADDICTION

*If Everton were playing at the bottom of
my garden, I'd shut the curtains.*

BILL SHANKLY

Watching football on the TV: it's an institution. Billions of people round the world spend countless hours glued to the action, whether huddled round small sets or big screens, whether at home, at a friend's or in the pub.

Today, we're inundated with choice when it comes to catching a game; it's not just a wealth of domestic matches that we can watch – we can settle in for 90 minutes of action from countless competitions taking place almost anywhere in the world. But it wasn't always thus.

Trying to tune in

For anyone over 40, it doesn't seem that long ago that watching an English top-tier game live on the box was something of a luxury, with fans at the mercy of the financial demands of club chairmen and television executives, and that catching a European game that wasn't the final was a testament to your ability to stay up late into the night, and your capacity to first endure the latest greyhound racing, showjumping or snooker action.

Watching World Cup games for this generation was different too: it was once the height of exoticism. Unreliable feeds from faraway lands beamed the jaw-dropping skills of unknown players directly into your living room. These matches really were a portal to another world: it was a thrill to be watching regardless of who was playing. The mix of excitement and curiosity of something so familiar yet so different was electrifying. These games were an education, a cultural event.

Of course, it's different now, thanks in no small part to Rupert Murdoch and Sky. His investment has transformed the way we watch football, from the way we tune in for live games and highlights to how we get the latest news and how we keep up with the latest scores.

The change in how we keep abreast of the goals rattling in on a Saturday afternoon is an apt illustration of the revolution that has occurred in televised football over the past 20 years. In the UK, we went from relying on Ceefax or Teletext, whose analogue technology had to be manually mined for updates, to Sky's all-singing and all-dancing *Soccer Saturday* phenomenon, with its panel of ex-pros discussing games that they can see but we can't, and its live updates from every ground in the country.

A history of football on TV

1937	The first televised match in England: Arsenal v. Arsenal Reserves
1938	The first televised international match: England v. Scotland
1938	The first televised FA Cup final: Huddersfield Town v. Preston North End
1955	The BBC launches its highlights show *Sports Special*
1960	The first live game is televised by ITV: Blackpool v. Bolton Wanderers
1962	*Match of the Week* and *Shoot* highlight programmes appear on ITV
1964	*Match of the Day* debuts on BBC2
1968	*The Big Match* is unveiled by London Weekend Television
1966	The BBC and ITV show the World Cup final live
1969	The first colour edition of *Match of the Day* is broadcast
1970	The first Goal of the Month competition appears
1970	Chelsea v Leeds United attracts a record audience of 20 million viewers

1970	The first World Cup (in Mexico) is shown in colour
1971	Slow-motion replays are introduced
1983	The first live league game is shown since 1960: Tottenham Hotspur v. Nottingham Forest
1992	The Premier League is formed and BSkyB buy the rights to show the games
1992	ITV starts screening live Champions League football
1992	Channel 4 begin showing live Italian Serie A football
1997	The first channel dedicated to a single club football is launched by Manchester United: MUTV
2003	Sky and ITV share Champions League football coverage
2004	Sunday night *Match of the Day 2* is launched by the BBC
2010	The first live Premier League game in 3D is screened by Sky
2013	The Champions League final draws a TV audience of 360 million
2015	Champions League and Europa League football will be exclusively screened by BT Sport

The voice of football

Part of the fabric of football on the TV is the commentators. Their prose can be as memorable as the game they're describing; it can be what makes it memorable. There is no better example than the Kenneth Wolstenholme  commentary on the 1966 World Cup final between England and West Germany. If you're English, regardless of the generation you belong to, his famous words, 'Some people are on the pitch… they think it's all over… it is now!', will forever be a reminder of English football's most glorious moment. These ones from Wolstenholme have just as much power: 'It is only twelve inches high… it is solid gold… and it undeniably means England are the champions of the world.'

Another one of Britain's football commentary greats is Brian Moore, whose injection of the words 'It's up for grabs now… ' into the dying seconds of the battle for the 1989 first division title, in which Arsenal would score to dramatically snatch the crown from Liverpool's grasp, brilliantly defined the stomach-turning tension of what was unfolding before him and something that would become part of football folklore.

Of course, every country has its own favourites. When Bjørge Lillelien uttered the immortal words in 1981 on Norwegian television, 'Lord Nelson! Lord Beaverbrook! Sir Winston Churchill! Sir Anthony Eden! Clement Attlee! Henry Cooper! Lady Diana! Maggie Thatcher – can you hear me, Maggie Thatcher! Your boys took one hell of a beating! Your boys took one hell of a beating!', the popular commentator left no doubt as to how the Norwegians felt to beat England. His outburst made him a hero, and not just in his native land: there are quite a few Scots who take great pleasure in remembering his words.

Footie Fact

In 2007, Jacqui Oatley became the first woman to commentate on a football game on Match of the Day, *describing the Premier League match between Fulham and Blackburn Rovers.*

Game time

Of course, we do more than just watch football on the screen; we play it as well. Today the football video games industry is a multi-billion-pound business; a high-tech 3D world of playing and managing that features real players and real-life action. It's a far cry from the first games played on the likes of the Atari, ZX Spectrum or Commodore 64 in the 1980s.

When it came to playing on the ZX Spectrum, getting to the start was an art of perseverance in itself, involving carefully loading the game, which meant inserting a tape into a cassette deck and waiting for what seemed like an eternity for the basic graphics to appear. If you bumped the tape player, you had to start the whole process again. And when it did load, decent action was at a premium – the early games were more about managing a team, with any playing options incredibly basic by today's standards. Yet for football-obsessed kids, they were still gripping and an enthralling way to while away hour after hour.

Of course, the advent of technology only made football games more exciting. With the arrival of new computer systems, such as the Amiga and Nintendo, so arcade-style playing of football became possible, which for those used to rudimentary games, was a watershed moment. Fast forward and now the likes of the *FIFA* and *Pro Evolution Soccer* series, which are played on a host of consoles including the Nintendo Wii and 3DS, the PS4 and PSP, and the Xbox 360 and Xbox One, bestride the football video game world like giants, with adults as much as kids the main players.

The *Football Manager* title remains amazingly popular, showing that football fans are as eager to hone their management skills as they are their playing, especially if it means having the chance to lead your lower-league team to the type of domestic and European glory that would be out of reach in the real world. The technology and scope of the game has evolved incredibly since the days when the likes of Bryan Robson and Kenny Dalglish were favourite players, with its realism such that some diehard gamers have applied for actual football management positions. They didn't get them of course, but the joy of game: it's right there.

Footie Fact

According to the Guinness World Records, the record for the longest football video game marathon is 38 hours, 49 minutes and 13 seconds, set by Portuguese pair Marco Ramos and Efraim Ie on Pro Evolution Soccer 2012 *in November 2011.*

1981 – Atari launches *Pelé's Soccer*

1982 – The first *Football Manager* is available for the ZX Spectrum

1989 – *Kick Off* and its arcade-style action arrives on the Amiga

1992 – *Championship Manager* become a favourite on the PC

1993 – *Sensible Soccer* makes a play for *Kick Off*'s crown

1994 – 2D football with *International Superstar Soccer* for the SNES

1994 – The first 3D football with *Virtua Striker*

1995 – Multi-player games are possible thanks to *Actua Soccer*

1997 – *Premiership Manager 98* lets users manage a Premiership team

1998 – *FIFA Road to World Cup 98* is licensed by FIFA

2001 – *Pro Evolution Soccer* makes its debut on the PS2

2013 – *FIFA 14, Pro Evolution Soccer 2014* and *Football Manager 2014* take a bow

FOOTBALL PLAYERS: THE BEST OF THE BEST

Maradona good, Pelé better, George Best.
FOOTBALL SAYING IN BELFAST, BIRTHPLACE OF GEORGE BEST

Trying to pick the best players isn't easy – just look at the state of a lot of fantasy football teams. Nevertheless it's something we're keen to do and we're not alone. Football loves a trophy and the game's governing bodies love to give them out, and the world's best player is an obvious accolade to reward. However, the prize is a relatively new one, a status that shows just how recent the globalisation of the game has been.

A golden ball

In the beginning, there was a golden ball, the Ballon D'Or, a prize for the European Footballer of the Year conceived in 1956 by French football journalist Gabriel Hanot, shortly after he helped establish the European Cup, the forerunner of today's Champions League empire.

The prize was voted for by journalists and was only open to European players appearing for European clubs. So, the likes of Pelé, Garrincha and Jairzinho weren't included. Nevertheless, the list of early winners still reads like a roll call of the world's greatest players.

The criteria changed in 1995 to include non-European players at clubs in Europe and then in 1997 to any player in the world, at which point the Ballon D'Or became a world's best player trophy in all but name. Unsurprisingly, South Americans became frequent winners. However, by this time, FIFA had got in on the act and launched its own World Player of the Year award, as voted for by the coaches and captains of international teams. While undoubtedly a lofty honour, the FIFA award, initially at least, didn't have the glamour of its more established counterpart. That said, its cachet did rise and in 2010 common sense broke out, with the organisers of the two awards deciding to throw their lots in together and create the FIFA Ballon D'Or. Football had a singular award to recognise the best player on

the planet. So far the battle for ownership of this stellar bauble has been a straight fight between Argentina and Portugal, with the combat taking place largely in Spain.

On top of the world

The world's best player winner's board is currently dominated by Barcelona's Argentinian wizard Lionel Messi and Real Madrid's Portuguese wonder boy Cristiano Ronaldo. The last time anyone else won any of the top player awards was 2007. Messi alone has won the FIFA Ballon D'Or three times and the FIFA gong and the old-school Ballon D'Or once in that time.

Back in those dim, distant days before Messi and Ronaldo made the award shows all a bit samey, multiple wins were a little thinner on the ground. This brings us neatly to the original Ronaldo (Ronaldo Luís Nazário de Lima), the Brazilian centre forward whose hearty appetite has become clear since he retired. In his trimmer days, he scored goals and bagged awards for fun, including the FIFA–Ballon D'Or double in 1997 and 2002. Another all-time great to notch up this double header was Zinedine Zidane, in 1998. He went on to win the FIFA award again in 2000 and 2003
– he may have bowed out, in more ways than one, with a single header (to the chest of Italian defender Marco Materazzi), but he was undoubtedly the greatest player of his generation and possibly a few others.

Before 1991, there was only one trophy available and repeat winners in this era were even rarer, which makes the feats of three-time Ballon D'Or victors Johan Cruyff, Michel Platini and Marco van Basten even more impressive. Can you separate these players? Not really, but van Basten also took home the second FIFA award in 1992, while Platini won the Ballon D'Or three years on the trot between 1983 and 1985. Which leaves Cruyff, and it wouldn't be right to put him at the bottom of this exclusive pile. Let's just say that he is one of the greatest players in the history of the game.

As for players who got their hands on the ultimate award twice, the roll call is just as glittering. The list includes Argentinian-cum-Colombian-cum-Spaniard Alfredo di Stéfano, whose eagerness for passports eventually qualified him; Franz Beckenbauer, or 'Der Kaiser' to his compatriots and quite a few others; and Karl-Heinz Rummenigge, a scoring machine and perpetual trophy winner of the type Germany seems to produce regularly.

Most Ballon D'or/ FIFA Ballon D'or Wins by Club

Barcelona (Spain)

Juventus (taly)

Milan (Milan)

Real Madrid (Spain)

Bayern Munich (Germany)

Manchester United (England)

Dynamo Kyiv (Ukraine)

Internazionale (Italy)

Hamburg (Germany)

Blackpool (England)

Dukla Prague (Czech Republic)

Dynamo Moscow (Russia)

Benfica (Portugal)

Ferencváros (Hungary)

Ajax (Netherlands)

Borussia Mönchengladbach (Germany)

Marseille (France)

Borussia Dortmund (Germany)

Liverpool (England)

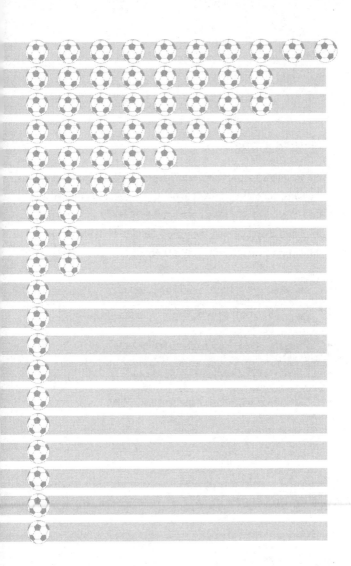

One-time winners

There are only a few countries for which producing world-class players is the norm rather than the exception. Just as Germany, Netherlands, France, Brazil and Italy have been hotbeds of talent and, as a result, world's best player awards, there are a handful of nations that have had the chance to celebrate a winner only once.

- Bulgaria – 1994, Hristo Stoichkov, Barcelona

- Denmark – 1997, Allen Simonsen, Borussia Mönchengladbach

- Hungary – 1967, Flórián Albert, Ferencváros

- Liberia – 1995, George Weah, AC Milan

- Ukraine – 2004, Andriy Shevchenko, AC Milan

The best of British

It started so well: the first Ballon D'Or was awarded to an Englishman: Stanley Matthews. After the hubris-hammering defeats to the USA at the 1950 World Cup and, more notably, at the hands of Ferenc Puskás' Hungary in 1953 and 1954, the English FA were no doubt over the moon to see English football back on top again. And the Blackpool outside right was a worthy winner: he is considered one of the greatest English exponents of the game and even at 38 in 1956, he still had another 12 years of professional football to play.

England had to wait ten years for another stellar performer, in World Cup winner Bobby Charlton, but the Scots didn't have to be quite so patient, with Manchester United's Denis Law voted top of pile in 1964. Another Red Devil, George Best, made it three British winners in five years, claiming the gong in 1967 on the back of his club side's triumph in the European Cup. Thereafter British football has had little to cheer about: its 'Best' days were quite literally behind it, in terms of world's best player awards at least. Kevin Keegan did win back-to-back titles in the late 1970s, albeit playing for German team Hamburg, and the only British winner since was Liverpool's Michael Owen in 2001.

Will Britain have another champion to celebrate soon? The chances aren't great: Scotland and Northern Ireland are looking better at a national level after some tough times, but both lack world-class players. As for England, is Wayne Rooney a candidate? Many feel that his moment has passed. And then there's Wales, which has no winners to hold aloft as a symbol of its footballing pedigree. However, if any Brit is going to walk away with the trophy soon it will most likely be a Welshman; Real Madrid's Gareth Bale.

Footie Fact

France Football devised a Player of the Century award in 1999. The award, voted for by the previous Ballon D'Or winners, went to Pelé. Maradona came second and Johan Cruyff third.

CHAPTER 14

AROUND THE WORLD IN FOOTBALL TOURNAMENTS

A chap was once trying to get me to play for his club in America. 'We'll pay you $20,000 this year,' he said, 'and $30,000 next year.' 'OK,' I replied, 'I'll sign next year.'

GEORGE BEST

One of the great football debates is 'what is the best league in the world?'. Is it the English Premier League? The Spanish La Liga? The German Bundesliga? The Italian Serie A or the French Ligue 1? But why stop there? Is the UEFA Champions League better than the African or South American equivalents? And what about international competitions? How does the European Championship stack up against the Africa Cup of Nations or the Copa América?

League rivalry

Let's start with domestic football and assume that because Europe attracts the world's best players (based on the fact that European club players dominate world's best player awards), its top leagues are the best in the world. So, is it really possible to choose between them? The French league is certainly the *arriviste*: for a long time it existed in the shadow of its continental peers, but a colossal injection of cash from Qatari and Russian billionaires has put it in a new light. The face of French football is very different thanks to the newly minted Paris Saint-Germain and AS Monaco.

But football teams having extraordinary amounts of money is not exactly a new phenomenon in European club football. The number of wealthy foreign investors in the English Premier League grows season by season, with this charge of the billionaire brigade led by Chelsea's very own oligarch Roman Abramovich and continued by, among others, Abu Dhabi's Sheikh Mansour at Manchester City and the American Glazer family at Old Trafford. As for Italy, Indonesian tycoon Erick Thohir took over Inter Milan in 2013. Perhaps the lack of mega-rich foreign owners is what sets Spanish and German football apart, for now at least, although Barcelona and Real Madrid are among the richest clubs in the world and throw their weight around in the transfer market accordingly: just look at Madrid's love for *galácticos*.

RAY HAMILTON

THE JOY OF GOLF

THE JOY OF CRICKET

Graham Tarrant

ISBN: 978 1 84953 599 1   Hardback   £9.99

I am confident they play cricket in heaven. Wouldn't be heaven otherwise, would it?

PATRICK MOORE

This pocket-sized miscellany, packed with fascinating facts, amusing anecdotes and captivating stories and quotes from the world of cricket, is perfect for anyone who knows the incomparable joy of the gentleman's game.

THE JOY OF CRICKET

GRAHAM TARRANT

THE JOY OF RUGBY

Steven Gauge

ISBN: 978 1 84953 601 1   Hardback   £9.99

The whole point of rugby is that it is, first and foremost, a state of mind, a spirit.

Jean-Pierre Rives

This pocket-sized miscellany, packed with fascinating facts, amusing anecdotes and captivating stories and quotes from the world of rugby, is perfect for anyone who knows the incomparable joy of picking up the ball and running with it.

STEVEN GAUGE

Footie Fact

The last team outside of Manchester and London to win the top prize in English domestic football was Blackburn Rovers in 1995. The top scorer that season: Rovers' Alan Shearer with 34 goals.

As for the German Bundesliga: Bayern Munich are undoubtedly a heavyweight but for the time being there isn't the same level of foreign money and it is notable that it is usually only Bayern that splash fantastic amounts of cash on players. Tellingly, the Bundesliga is famous for its low ticket prices.

How about styles of play? The English Premier League is known for its frenetic pace and valuing industry over ability. The English game is also renowned for its physicality. Anyone who has grown up playing football in England and then taken to the field in Europe, at whatever level, will know that competing requires less muscularity and less contact.

The pace of football in Spain and Italy is traditionally slower, which when combined with the reduced physicality, supposedly gives a greater platform for players' technical ability. Just a stereotype? Well, look at the garlands Barcelona and Spain's possession-based game *tika-taka* has received. Where does French and German football stand in all of this? Somewhere in between, with the former perhaps displaying a more continental style and the latter closer in complexion to the English game. However, as football comes increasingly to resemble one giant melting pot, with domestic leagues featuring players from every corner of the planet and with the idea of nationality and different nations' styles being subverted not only by this distribution of talent but also the multinational heritage of a growing number of young players, these lines will blur further and it will be harder to apply any stereotypes. That said, the arguments are likely to go on just the same.

Continental shifts

If the UEFA Champions League is the Hollywood blockbuster that everyone and his dog knows about, the Copa Libertadores, the South American equivalent, is the indie star that despite being blessed with unbelievable quality can struggle to find a global audience. And what does that make the African Champions League? The arthouse oddity? The no-budget surprise?

One thing is for certain when it comes to the African Champions League; while it may not have the riches, global viewing figures or all-star cast of its more illustrious compatriots, it is no less competitive or colourful. What challenges does the UEFA competition throw up for players? Well, for big-club players there are the occasional trips to smaller teams from less celebrated leagues whose changing rooms and pitches aren't as manicured as the ones they're used to, and for those not used it, playing in inclement conditions in the outreaches of Eastern Europe must be something of an inconvenience. Also, there's the reality of playing important domestic games after just a

couple of days rest. When it comes to the African Champions League, concerns are a little different. First of all, flying across Europe in club jets or those chartered from British Airways or the like is one thing, but criss-crossing Africa on airlines with less reassuring safety records is another altogether. Then there's the prevalence of war in Africa, which affects everything from travel and accommodation, to pitch conditions and the stability of spectators. Can you imagine how England, Spain or Italy's top players would deal with the need for 12-hour flying schedules to avoid warzones or armed soldiers running on the pitch to confront them about a tackle? Or how about voodoo in the form of blood sprinkled under seats? Or, thanks to rules that say home teams are responsible for the opposition's accommodation, having to stay in a hotel located in a red-light district whose noise prohibits rest for even the deepest of sleepers? Winning the UEFA Champions League is the ultimate test of a team? It's hard not to read about the African Champions League and think otherwise.

International battle

When it comes to regional international tournaments, the European Championship, the Africa Cup of Nations and the Copa América are the big ones. Being champions of Europe, Africa or South America is as big as it sounds.

The Copa América arguably has the grandest game of them all: Brazil against Argentina, a clash whose history and talented combatants rarely make it anything other than explosive. Getting one over on the old enemy means as much in South America as it does anywhere else. That's not to the say the rest of the teams are makeweights: Uruguay are frequent apple-cart upsetters, winning the tournament in 2011 and holding the record for most trophies going into the 2015 competition, and the regular inclusion of top teams from Central and North America, such as Mexico and the USA, also keeps things interesting.

The big guns in the Africa Cup of Nations are the likes of Egypt, Nigeria, Cameroon, Ghana and the Ivory Coast. Between them, this group has taken the trophy home on 19 occasions since the first tournament in 1957, with Egypt the top dog by some distance with seven victories, including three in a row in the 2000s. But that doesn't mean the title hasn't been shared around: only as recently as 2012, when the competition was held in Gabon and Equatorial Guinea, the unfancied Zambia team beat favourites Ivory Coast 8–7 on penalties in the final. David beat Goliath.

As for the European Championship, Spain have had a stranglehold on this trophy for a while now, winning in 2008 and 2012, but this competition has thrown up its fair share of surprises in the past 20 years or so. When Denmark were drafted in at the last minute to replace Yugoslavia in 1992, no one expected the Danes, many of whom were in holiday mode, to walk away with the title. But they did and they beat the mighty Germany in the final too. Three tournaments and 12 years later, Greece ripped up the form book and beat hot favourites and hosts Portugal in the final. The football might not have been pretty but the Greeks didn't care: the records show they were European champions. Which is more than England can claim.

Footie Fact

Who is the European Championship's top goal scorer? Former French midfielder and current UEFA President Michel Platini, who scored nine goals in a single tournament in 1984. Who can catch him? All eyes on Cristiano Ronaldo if Portugal make France 2016.

CHAPTER 15

LIFE AFTER FOOTBALL

Tell him he's Pelé and get him back on.

PARTICK THISTLE MANAGER JOHN LAMBIE ON BEING TOLD BY THE PHYSIO THAT HIS STRIKER COLIN MCGLASHAN HAD SUFFERED CONCUSSION AND DIDN'T KNOW WHO HE WAS

A life without football: a chilling thought if there ever was one. For players, even the longest careers have to come to an end. And then what? Naturally, football being football, just because a player is retired doesn't mean there isn't an interest in what they're up to. The decision to swap playing for managing retains a timeless popularity, but if a footballer is loath to stray too far from pitchside, today there are other options: never have the professions of commentator, pundit and presenter been so populated with former players. But once, it wasn't the commentator's microphone or the pundits chair that most appealed, but the other side of the bar, with owning a pub a much preferred retirement plan. Of course, there are those who bucked the trend.

The longest footballing careers

Whether Arsène Wenger deserves all the credit or not, footballer's careers are much longer today thanks to the change in attitude to eating and drinking that he, at the very least, helped introduce. From the mid-1990s, when the French manager took charge of Arsenal, discussion of footballers' diets no longer focused solely on industrial quantities of lager and steak and chips.

Gradually it became acceptable to talk about pasta, steamed meat, vegetables and rice, and having only the occasional beer. Today, strict diets are part and parcel of a top player's life – you read about Ryan Giggs giving up butter on his toast to help extend his playing career – and being teetotal, at least during the season, is increasingly common. In the modern Premier League era, turning up to training smelling like a brewery is an offence that will most likely find you dropped and fined, but you don't need to go back too many years to find tales of players kicking off while half-cut. It isn't much wonder that careers were much shorter in the days before Wenger.

Giggs is a good example of this revolution. The beginning of the 2013–14 season was the 23rd for the Welsh Wizard, who celebrated his 40th birthday not long into it. He has one more to go to match Paolo Maldini, who retired at 41 having played 24 seasons for AC Milan and Italy, and won a mantelpiece full of top honours. Other receivers of notable long-service awards include Maldini's teammate Franco Baresi, a sweeper for 20 years at the Rossoneri; Francesco Totti, who has been playing in Serie A for AS Roma's first team for 22 years; Jack Charlton, who shored up Leeds United's defence between 1953 and 1972; and Paul Scholes, who drove Manchester United's midfield for 20 years from 1993 to 2013.

However, none of them can match Stanley Matthews, whose senior playing career spanned 37 years, with the famous outside right competing at the top level until 1965 when he was 50. It can't be a coincidence that the Magician, as he was known, was teetotal, a vegetarian and a non-smoker.

Footie Fact

Former goalkeeper Peter Shilton made 1,390 appearances during his career, which included 1,005 league games in England. He also holds the record number of England caps, at 125.

Football boots to manager's suits

Swapping the pitch for the dugout has long been a chosen career path for players throughout the game, and time has shown that brilliance with the ball still remains no indicator of managerial aptitude. That's not to say the efforts of these institutionalised souls haven't added something joyful to the game, whether they've flourished or failed.

Roy Keane isn't everyone's cup of tea, but he is universally regarded as one of the best players of his generation. A midfield maestro and menace combined in one gloriously effective footballer. Yet managerial life hasn't been kind to him: it all started so well at Sunderland before ending in barbed comments and resignation amid a run of poor results. And the less said about his tenure at Ipswich Town the better. Another outstanding footballer unable to match success on the pitch to that off it is Holland's Ruud Gullit, whose prowess on the field earned an incredible haul of medals but whose ability in the dugout hasn't been so illustrious, including being sacked by Chelsea and Newcastle United.

But failing to transfer mastery on the field to success in the manager's seat is by no means a modern phenomenon. Step forward World Cup-winning hero Sir Bobby Charlton, who took up a role of player–manager at Preston North End after his time at Manchester United. He steered the team to relegation in his first season and it wasn't long after that he thought better of management altogether, never to take up such a role again.

Of the top footballers that have made a success of management, perhaps the best advertisement for the ex-player is Pep Guardiola. While his managerial star is burning the brightest of all at the moment, making Bayern Munich even more imperious after leading Barcelona to unprecedented success, it shouldn't be forgotten that before he stepped into his manager's shoes, his boots were helping to orchestrate the midfield at the Camp Nou.

Another star player–star manager is Carlo Ancelotti. At club level he captained Roma to an Italian championship and four Coppa Italia trophies, and at AC Milan, he was part of one of the best teams of the time, winning back-to-back European Cups in 1989 and 1990 alongside the likes of Marco van Basten, Ruud Gullit, Frank Rijkaard, Paolo Maldini and Franco Baresi. Incredibly, his managerial career has been even more glittering, winning top-flight league championships in the Premier League, Serie A and Ligue 1 with Chelsea, AC Milan and Paris Saint-Germain respectively, as well as two Champions Leagues with the Italian team. Having stepped into the managerial hot seat at Real Madrid in 2013, only a fool would bet against him adding to his illustrious haul.

Unusual retirements

When they hang up their boots, not all footballers follow the path into the managerial or media worlds. A few have ended up in some more unusual post-career professions. If anything, knowing that some players end up doing more ordinary jobs makes them all the more likable, a bit more like one of us.

Perhaps the most famous member of this club is former Swedish international Tomas Brolin. Known once to his country and Leeds United fans as a striking wunderkind, his reputation has rather been taken over by his exploits in retirement. He has been involved in selling shoes, vacuum cleaners and properties in Sweden, and has tried his hand at being a restaurateur, as well as making a pop record with 1990s flash-in-the-pan Dr Alban. Staying in Scandinavia, former Danish international PSV Eindhoven player Ivan Nielsen decided to become a plumber, while Brolin's fellow Swede and ex-Sheffield Wednesday star Klas Ingesson chose a life as a lumberjack.

English football is full of such stories as well. England World Cup winner Ray Wilson worked as an undertaker when he gave up the game and former England midfielder Neil Webb became a postman on retirement. More recently, ex-journeyman striker Brett Angell spent some time stacking shelves at a well-known supermarket (before going on to coach in New Zealand). Clearly, every little helped. Of course, a retirement job out of the game doesn't always mean one out of the glare of the camera and press. Eric Cantona swapped

the Theatre of Dreams for treading actual boards, appearing in films including *Elizabeth* and *Looking for Eric*. If the transformation of the enigmatic Frenchman from star player to film star didn't surprise too many, the same move by footballing hard man Vinnie Jones certainly did. Indeed, he has arguably found more success in front of the camera than in front of a back four, with roles in *Lock, Stock and Two Smoking Barrels*, *Snatch* and *X-Men: The Last Stand* to name but a few. Football: it's a funny old game.

What is a club in any case? Not the buildings or the directors or the people who are paid to represent it. It's not the television contracts, get-out clauses, marketing departments or executive boxes. It's the noise, the passion, the feeling of belonging, the pride in your city. It's a small boy clambering up stadium steps for the very first time, gripping his father's hand, gawping at that hallowed stretch of turf beneath him and, without being able to do a thing about it, falling in love.

SIR BOBBY ROBSON